MW00436205

BECOMING EZRA JACK KEATS

BECOMING
EZRA JACK KEATS

VIRGINIA MCGEE BUTLER

UNIVERSITY PRESS OF MISSISSIPPI ∾ JACKSON

Willie Morris Books in Memoir and Biography

The University Press of Mississippi is the scholarly publishing agency of
the Mississippi Institutions of Higher Learning: Alcorn State University,
Delta State University, Jackson State University, Mississippi State University,
Mississippi University for Women, Mississippi Valley State University,
University of Mississippi, and University of Southern Mississippi.

www.upress.state.ms.us

The University Press of Mississippi is a member
of the Association of University Presses.

First printing 2023
∞

Library of Congress Cataloging-in-Publication Data available

LCCN 2022048800
ISBN 9781496844743 (hardcover)
ISBN 9781496844750 (epub single)
ISBN 9781496844767 (epub institutional)
ISBN 9781496844774 (pdf single)
ISBN 9781496844781 (pdf institutional)

British Library Cataloging-in-Publication Data available

To Martin and Lillie Pope, who encouraged Ezra to follow his dreams, and to Allen Butler, who has encouraged me to follow mine

CONTENTS

PREFACE

THE FOLLOWING ACCOUNT DRAWS HEAVILY ON KEATS'S AUTO-biography, which he wrote much as he told stories in conversations, with one episode reminding him of something else—often from a totally different time period. It comes largely from Keats's tapes and writings but is tempered by articles about him in newspapers and magazines and by the view of those who knew him and his family. Using all these resources, I have put this biography together much like a jigsaw puzzle.

I did my primary research at the de Grummond Children's Literature Collection at the University of Southern Mississippi (USM). The Keats archives in this collection include an extensive assortment of memorabilia, artifacts, correspondence, newspaper and magazine clippings, and paintings from Ezra's life and those invaluable drafts of his unfinished and unpublished autobiography. I am grateful to the Ezra Jack Keats Foundation and the de Grummond Children's Literature Collection for making this available and for their encouragement in my own winding pathway through his archives to find his story.

An interesting question arose early in my research, "Was this author/artist 'Ezra' or 'Jack'?" Answers varied. I asked Jeannine Laughlin-Porter, the Children's Book Festival Director in March

1980 when Ezra Jack Keats came to USM in Hattiesburg to receive the USM Medallion for his body of work as a children's author and illustrator. She answered quickly, "Oh, we always called him Jack." Author Brian Alderson begins his book *Ezra Jack Keats: Artist and Picture-Book Maker*, "He was not Ezra Jack Keats to begin with, but Jacob Ezra Katz, known to everyone as Jack."

However, Dr. Deborah Pope, director of the Ezra Jack Keats Foundation and daughter of his lifelong friend Martin, gave a different and definitive answer: "We always called him Ezra."

When I began this research, I already knew that Keats had led a new writing trend, bringing children from many cultures into an almost all-white world of picture books. I had used his books with my classes when I taught kindergarten and second grade. Commissioned to examine his life and works for the fiftieth-anniversary edition of *The Snowy Day*, I pictured children and teachers who loved his books becoming fascinated with his story. As I did the research, another question became bigger than what to call him: "Who was the man who owned the name?"

My reading included books and magazine articles about him, his autobiographical writings, and his accumulated correspondence. I listened to his taped interviews and talked to people who knew him, including two delightful phone conversations with his best friends Martin and Lillie Pope. During the time we spent together at the Kaigler Children's Book Festival, Deborah Pope and I became friends. I heard bits and pieces of Keats's life remembered by these people who knew him well.

In his memories, Ezra often recalled hard times and sadness. He remembered himself as a lonely child in an unhappy family. Others remembered his talent, his sense of humor, and a family that welcomed visitors and found occasions for joy despite living in difficult times. In telling his story, I came back to the question of what to call him. He is addressed in letters in his correspondence files as both Jack and Ezra. Like many people, he went by two names. Most often "Ezra" occurs with those who knew him at home and in his neighborhood, with "Jack" starting in his school setting and continuing in his working life. In this book, I have called him by both names—using the one he would likely have been called at that time and place.

Learning and writing the Keats story has been an adventure. I never met Ezra Jack Keats, yet I count myself a close friend. I call him Ezra.

BECOMING EZRA JACK KEATS

CHAPTER 1

SHAKY START

Art and Illness

EXPLAINING HIS ABILITY TO CONNECT WITH CHILDREN, EZRA Jack Keats said, "I really am an ex-kid. All you need is a good memory." One might argue that the "ex" is nondescriptive but that the kid permeated the adult and eventually his stories. An excerpt from "My Heart Leaps Up" by William Wordsworth may be more accurate in describing the relationship of Keats's childhood to his body of work:

> So was it when my life began;
> So is it now I am a man:
> So be it when I shall grow old . . .
> The Child is father of the man.

Keats's perceived childhood memories informed his depiction of both the children in his stories and the adults who interacted with them. He took what he saw as injustice to his inner ex-kid, rectified it, and portrayed family and friendship in an idealized world that he believed every child should experience. Starting at the beginning brings understanding of the purposefulness in his body of work, which includes but goes beyond the joy of reading good picture books.

Jacob Ezra Katz was born 11 March 1916. His family called him "Ezra," which means teacher or helper, a hopeful name for a rather scrawny baby who remained in an incubator at the hospital until he gained strength. His father brought him home to a railroad flat on Vermont Street in Brooklyn, where one room ran into the next like cars on a train and stood beside another family railroad flat just like it. Neighbors came to check out the new baby: "Boy, is he skinny! Do you think he'll make it?"

"Watch," said Mr. Katz. Everybody hushed and gazed as Ezra grabbed when his father held his thumbs above Ezra's head. "See! That rascal with the spaghetti fingers is pulling himself up. See how strong he is!"

Ezra always remembered his father telling him a special story about his birth, claiming that an angel came from heaven and told Ezra all the secrets of life. Then the angel made a dent with his finger in Ezra's chin, giving him a permanent cleft to remind him to keep the secrets. Sometimes his father ended the story wistfully, "You must know things I don't." As Ezra listened to the story, he thought he could remember the brush of huge angel wings. Afterward, his father sang songs to him until he went to sleep.

Ezra claimed other memories of lying in bed facing the window that looked out over three-story tenement buildings. Bright sunlight shone on the ropes where people hung their wash. His vivid recollection of bright reds and stark whites flapping in the breeze framed by the window served as a metaphoric prediction of his first paintings.

The Katz family's precarious place in the world began in Poland's capital city of Warsaw in the late nineteenth century, long before Ezra was born. Ezra's orphaned father Benjamin had been adopted in Poland by a well-to-do uncle. When he got out of hand in 1883 as a teenager, the uncle shipped him off to America.

His mother Augusta's family, the Podgainys, locked themselves inside their house when mob rioters in the Polish pogroms came for them. Augusta, who went by the nickname Gussie, heard a priest begging the crowd to stop and go away above the noise that raged just outside their door. The mob knocked him down and continued their destruction. Then she heard their landlord, a Polish Christian: "Anyone who comes through this door is going to have his head chopped off!" The landlord brandished his ax until everybody left.

Needing to find safety, the Podgainys joined immigrants from many nations who came to America in the late 1800s and early 1900s. Frank Leslie's *Illustrated Newspaper* reported that four thousand people entered the United States on the single day of 5 May 1891. Some came for freedom to express their political views and some for the adventure of a new world. In 1878, the Podgainys joined other Jewish families from Warsaw seeking an escape from persecution. These immigrants bought the cheapest tickets in the part of the ship below the waterline, the steerage, named for being close to the steering mechanism. They passed one medical exam in Poland and a second after standing in line with the mass of people awaiting their turns to be checked before boarding the ship.

Their world for the next two to three weeks was a packed space with the only light coming from the portholes. Beneath the portholes, narrow tables and benches were affixed with row after row of iron berths measuring eighteen inches wide by six feet long. The Podgainys crammed into the remaining space with many other passengers. One traveler's trip account describes women complaining in a high key while the men swore in twelve languages. A bit of light, ventilation, and sometimes water came through the portholes. Salted meats and fish, potatoes or rice, and pea or bean soup made up their scant meals. A sailor took pity on Gussie's sister Jenny and offered her a banana. She'd never seen one before, and she ate it—peel and all.

With the steerage getting the brunt of the rocking ocean, seasickness was common. Lice and various diseases passed from one passenger to the other in the close quarters. In some accounts 10–15 percent of the people died during the two- to three-week voyage, giving the nickname "coffin ships" to the immigrant vessels. Jenny did not live to complete the voyage.

Their ship landed on lower Manhattan with other challenges ahead for its passengers. First class and cabin passengers were let off at the pier, while travelers in steerage were held for another check against the ship's manifest and a third brief medical exam at Castle Garden before they could enter the United States. The inspections sought to eliminate any people likely to become public charges, carry contagious diseases, or become polygamists. Nervously, the Podgainys wondered if one of their family members would be among the 2 percent who were refused entrance and had to make the difficult return journey.

After all the family had their names checked against the ship's manifest and passed their last medical inspection, they went through customs and joined the group of immigrants who were piled into a horse-drawn wagon and taken to various addresses in upper sections of New York City where someone had vouched for them. Thirteen-year-old Gussie spoke not a word of English.

Both the Katz and Podgainy families settled in the New York borough of Brooklyn. The area had small communities of Jews, Slavs, and Greeks, with other cultures mixed among them. Their neighborhood had everything they needed—green grocers, butchers, a pharmacist for emergency first aid, and a candy store. Choices for worship on Saturdays or Sundays were a cathedral, a synagogue, and a storefront church. There was a deli with franks and delicious sandwiches where children might earn some unexpected change running errands.

These immigrant families brought their holidays, languages, religious observances, and traditions with them from their home countries. When the Katz and Podgainy families decided their children were old enough to get married, they found a matchmaker. The matchmaker paired Ben with Gussie, unconcerned about whether their personalities agreed with each other. They settled into the roles expected of a young married couple, with Ben working while Gussie cooked, cleaned, and cared for the children.

Gussie and Ben's first baby died. Mae, their second child, was born with a deformed spine. William was born next, and people called him "Kelly" because his red hair was the color of a favorite comic book character. Ezra came last. From the beginning, art and illness defined his life.

When he was a toddler, Ezra clutched a handful of crayons and scribbled designs all over the linoleum floor. When the crayons wore down to stubs, he ate them and their wrappings. Mrs. Katz was aghast. Snatching the crayons away and taking a spoonful of oatmeal, she held it to Ezra's mouth, but he clenched his teeth. "*Gotenyu*," she moaned, "why did you send me a baby that eats crayons instead of food?"

When he was four or five, one night he came into the kitchen and found an odd silence. Usually, his mother and father were there with Kelly or Mae, and often neighbors gathered. They talked, laughed, and had fun. Why was the kitchen quiet?

An open bottle of Waterman's blue-black ink and a pen on the big white table caught his eye. An overhead lightbulb threw Ezra's shadow across the table beside the pen and ink. He began to draw pigs, cats, dogs, and mice on the table. He added crooked little houses with smoke curling out of the chimneys. Moving around the table, he drew Indian heads with braids and feathers and Chinese people with big straw hats, copying stereotypes he saw all around him in advertising and magazines. Ezra forgot about the quiet as he drew zeppelins, airplanes, and ships with funnels pouring out lots of steam. He didn't stop until the table was covered.

Early the next morning, Ezra got up and stumbled into the kitchen to see his mother standing in her bathrobe staring at the table. "Did you do this?" she whispered.

Not knowing if he was in trouble, he thought fast. "I think so," he said.

His mother walked around the table examining the pictures. Finally, she said, "It's beautiful."

"Ya mean it?" he asked.

His mother left the room and came back with their only table-cloth, the one she saved for Sabbath dinners on Friday night. Carefully, she spread it over Ezra's art. "It's a shame to wash it off. This way it will last a while."

For nearly a week, the tablecloth saved the drawings. Every time a neighbor came over, Mrs. Katz took off the cloth. "Ezra's work," she bragged.

"Hmmm. So, Ezra did that," said the neighbors. When the pictures smeared and blurred, Ezra and Gussie reluctantly washed them off the table.

❧

Often, Ezra's stomach hurt, his nose ran, and he cried. Mrs. Katz wanted him to feel better, and she particularly wanted the crying to stop. "What do you want?" she would ask.

He didn't know how to explain, so he said, "I want a coloring book. I want crayons. I want orange Jell-O."

She bought him a coloring book and crayons. She made orange Jell-O and found enough coins in her husband's pockets to buy heavy cream to whip and put on the top. After Ezra colored the pictures and ate the Jell-O, his stomach still hurt, his nose ran, and he cried.

Once he had to go to the hospital. He brought his few, worn books, but the hospital made his mother take them back home. When he began to feel better, he asked his mother to bring him some new books. The next time she came, she brought a wrapped package. Ezra was excited until he opened it to find his same old books. How disappointed he was! He never thought that his mother might have been trying to make his old ones look better or that she might have been trying to keep the hospital from sending them home again.

$\mathcal{A}$T $\mathcal{H}$OME AND SCHOOL

EZRA USED HIS EARS AND EYES TO JUDGE A NEW WORLD WHEN he entered kindergarten. Children around him cried and clung to their mothers' skirts like they were going to jail. Their immigrant mothers wept, too, perhaps more frightened than the children. How could they leave their little ones in this strange environment with a teacher who spoke only English?

The teacher struggled to bring order in the chaos. She looked like a woman Ezra had seen in comic strips—an evil woman with black eyes, dark eyelashes, and straight black hair pulled back into a bun. She demanded that the children sit with their hands clasped in front of them on their ink-stained desks until time to use pens with points that broke and scraped. Ezra thought the splashes and scratches they made looked much like those he had seen in pictures of prison walls.

Officially, in more bad news, it appeared that Ezra must use Jacob, his first name, which was shortened to "Jack." For the rest of his life, he would switch back and forth between "Ezra" and "Jack." School papers and awards called him "Jack Katz." In adulthood, business papers and correspondence used Jack, but close friends and family most often called him Ezra.

Another change may have been even harder for him. His teacher's no-nonsense attitude allowed no time or patience in her schedule for activities like drawing pictures and painting. When his mother thought he needed to stay home because of his stomach problems or sinusitis, he took advantage of the opportunity and removed his broken crayons from a leftover red metal Swee-Touch-Nee tea chest. He arranged the crayon nubs, peeled the paper off as needed, and rubbed the broken pieces onto the paper. Jack, at school, kept his hands on his desk; Ezra, at home, painted crayon pictures.

Ezra copied and colored an American Indian from a nickel. From a coloring book, he traced two little girls who sat daintily in an unreal world with bows, dresses, and slippers. He told everybody he drew their pictures and basked in the praise, although he'd never seen any girls who looked like that. He didn't let this bit of cheating bother him but accepted their approval and gained confidence to do his own drawings.

Two teachers, women he would never forget, left entirely different impressions on him as he moved through elementary school. In class one day, someone hit Mrs. Houghton hard from behind with a spitball. She whirled around and looked deeply into the students' eyes to see who did it. Jack's face turned red.

"You did this!" she said.

"I didn't," said Jack. "I didn't."

"You are the only person whose face is red. It's obvious that you did it."

The episode imprinted itself on his mind and began an awareness of injustice. Whenever he saw judgments made on flimsy evidence, he always thought of Mrs. Houghton.

A happier memory came from Mrs. Hoffman's class, one that would reappear many years later. He cut out a paper silhouette the color of a sweet potato, glued it to a different sheet of paper, and brought it to her for a present. She hung it on the wall. At first, Jack thought she was just being nice to a little kid, but the next day it was still there. Days and weekends came and went with his picture still hanging in the room. He made more pictures, cutting out silhouettes of birds, dogs, and a shepherd. Mrs. Hoffman hung them all and never took them down. Most likely, the word "collage" was not included in the vocabulary of either student or teacher at this point, but Jack felt like he belonged in this class, in his desk, surrounded by his art.

At home, struggle hovered within the Katz family. Ezra thought Mae resented him and his brother for growing up straight and tall while her back remained bent. The doctors put her in traction and fitted her with a corset, but she refused to wear the painful apparatus.

Mae sat on Ezra's bed to sew, often dropping her sewing needles and pins. One day, Ezra sat on the bed to fly his handmade cardboard airplane covered with tin foil. He piloted it thorough the sky, buzzing over the blankets that served as mountains in the desert, and banked it to come in for a landing on the bed. Suddenly, pain shot through his thigh, causing him to lose control and crash-land the plane. He discovered a needle with a trailing black thread. When the experience repeated with needles and pins striking Ezra at unexpected times and in surprising places, he thought Mae planted them in his bed on purpose, never considering that the small apartment had few seating options for Mae to do her needlework or that losing needles and pins is commonplace for people who sew.

There were no pets in the Katz household and few in the neighborhood because pets must be fed, and food cost money. But there were animals: roaches, ants, mice, and rats. Someone in the family pondered the mystery of the most likely path to catch a mouse and adventurously put a tiny piece of cheese in the trap. When the trap snapped, the bravest member of the family, usually Ezra's father or Kelly, would open it, get rid of the mouse, and set it again.

Perhaps what Ezra wanted most in his family was for his voice to be heard, for his thoughts to be taken seriously, and for his humor to bring laughter. With Kelly six years older than Ezra and Mae still older, he thought they treated him like an annoying little brother, never listening to what he had to say. If Ezra cracked a joke at supper, Kelly would say, "You heard that somewhere" and would never admit that Ezra had thought of it himself.

At one time before Ezra was born, Mr. Katz had been a partner with a Mr. Krem in the restaurant business. For some reason, the partnership broke up, with Mr. Krem going on to become quite successful while Mr. Katz became a counterman in a diner named Pete's Coffee Pot. When times were hard, his parents would tell Ezra that Mr. Krem had come to see him when he was about a year old and said, "What a beautiful little boy. I'd love to adopt him." They followed up the story with the comment that it was too bad they didn't give him to Mr. Krem because he could be going to school in a chauffeur-driven limousine and would have everything. What Ezra heard in this story was not his chance at plenty but his parents' willingness to give him away.

Yom Kippur made Ezra uncomfortable as he skipped the fasting and heard the rabbis denouncing the younger generation for drifting away from God, but he enjoyed Passover, partly because it gave his father a chance to shine. The dishes were all changed from their regular tableware according to the Jewish custom, and his father sat in state at the head of the table on a pillow. His father hid the matzo and celebrated when Ezra found it by giving him a quarter or half-dollar. As the youngest child, Ezra asked the four traditional questions of the Seder meal, each accompanied by a glass of wine, and his father gave the traditional answers recalling the deliverance of the Israelites from Egypt. Mr. Katz opened the door a bit and poured a fifth glass of wine for Elijah. It was said that the prophet visited every home on the Seder night and would one day make the announcement of the coming of the Jewish Messiah. Ezra puzzled over how Elijah found their house, but he was almost sure the wine rocked a bit and the level in the glass went down.

Because he worked nights at Pete's Coffee Pot, Mr. Katz slept in the daytime. Mrs. Katz complained about his snoring and his sleeping with his shoes on, hanging off the end of the bed. He'd say, "They're not on the bed, are they?" before turning over to go back to sleep. She went through his father's pockets as he slept, looking for change. Ezra knew to be quiet and not wake his father up. This strained relationship between his parents contrasted sharply with comments from people who knew Mr. Katz in the community and talked about his sense of humor and how his words made them double up in laughter. Occasionally, Ezra experienced that side of his father when they walked together and he could watch his father's eyes twinkle as his face burst into a grin while he told a yarn.

Sometimes when night fell, a bit of peace came over the family. Ezra often lay on a cot near the heater. He watched as his parents ate oranges or tangerines and threw the peels on top of the stove to see the plump moist orange peels shrivel and darken and emit the smell of fragrant citrus. His father rocked in his chair and read the *Jewish Daily Forward* aloud while his mother sewed or darned socks. Ezra listened to the letters by people asking advice on daily life in America written to the editor, Abraham Cahan, who answered arguments about *de knippel*, a bit of change wives saved from their house money and kept in a knotted kerchief. He told them what to do about fears of the old-age home, obnoxious in-laws, and disrespectful children. Ezra thought it sounded easy to solve difficult problems in a few sentences. The words brought a time of peace to his own family, and with the calm came drowsiness and sleep.

The Katz family enjoyed entertaining, and weekends often brought a party night. Their living room had a chandelier with six lamps, each with a different color bulb. For these festive events, they turned on the lights and bought lots of cream soda and cake. The relatives and faithful and true friends from the old country, who were almost like family, came. Enrico Caruso sang *Aida* and Al Jolson belted out "The Jazz Singer" on the Victrola they had bought with a little extra money. There were Yiddish songs, "Cohen on the Telephone" telling funny stories, and one recording with nothing but laughter. Joining the others who chuckled or giggled along with it, Ezra laughed until he cried. Nobody seemed to care that the records had a scratchy sound. His mother became a gracious hostess for these gatherings, serving good food while his father entertained with funny anecdotes. For a while his parents and their friends had a respite from their hard times.

Ezra envied other children who ate radishes with rye bread and chomped down on crunchy green peppers while he was confined to a bland diet with his mother's efforts to fend off vomiting and diarrhea. Along with his chronic illnesses, Ezra was beset with chronic crying spells. By the time he was eight years old, Ezra's family thought he was old enough for the crying to stop. They clamored for solutions.

"Maybe he became nervouser from paintin' pictures," Uncle Louie suggested.

"He quit all that for some time now," his mother said. She turned to Ezra. "You got pencils, crayons, even paint. Why don't you make pictures anymore? Maybe it'll make you feel better."

Local doctors had diagnosed him as anemic or short in the shoulder but gave no solutions to the crying problem. The family decided Dr. Morrell, who had studied in Vienna, would have solutions. The doctor made a house call, listened to his mother's account of the crying spells, had Ezra strip to the waist, and gave him an examination. All the while, he listened to Mrs. Katz explain that her heart condition and varicose veins were caused by her son's birth. The doctor's face flushed, and Ezra thought he was angry when he asked Mrs. Katz what doctor had given that diagnosis. She mumbled, "I sort of figured it out myself." The doctor closed his bag and told Ezra to get dressed since he could find nothing wrong with him. Dr. Morrell looked around the room and noticed the paintings on the wall. Mrs. Katz said, "My son did those." He walked around the apartment studying the paintings, and his mother told Ezra to bring his others from the closet.

"Would you like to make a deal?" the doctor asked. "I like the little color sketch of the rooftops. If it's okay with you, I'll accept it as payment for the visit, but there's no prescription I can give you."

Uncle Louie came up with a different solution to his crying. "Maybe his body was entered by a dybbuk who's crying for something." A dybbuk, according to Jewish folklore, was a disembodied human spirit, one with unfinished reparations for sins, who wandered the earth looking for a living person to inhabit. Uncle Louie proposed swinging a dead chicken above Ezra's head while chanting prayers to entice the spirit into the chicken. Ezra visualized the chickens Aunt Rosa plucked in the butcher's shop and pictured towers of feathers swirling over his head. No chicken whirling for him.

"He's wasting away," his father said. "How about a Good Jew?" Perhaps he adhered to the belief that a Good Jew, a rabbi living a pure life devoid of evil, could banish a dybbuk from the new home it had found.

Ezra thought this was a strange solution, but a trip with his father brought curiosity and a bit of hope. They'd have to take the elevated train (the "El") up into the Bronx, where there were more Good Jews than anywhere in the world. Since he'd hardly been out of the neighborhood and had never ridden on the El, Ezra found the trip both scary and exciting. He didn't consider that his father might also be fearful of going into a new part of the city, nor did he wonder about the time and money his father was spending to try to make him well and happy.

At the El entrance, Ezra and his father walked up the stairs of a chalet-type structure, paid the woman in the cage two nickels, walked on past the potbelly stove through the turnstile, and sat to wait until their train rattled in. As they rode high above the city, Ezra decided they were as close to heaven as they were likely to get. He watched patterns cast by the sun, the shadow of the El, and complex grid works of iron and steel. Ezra peeked into people's houses and saw them looking back. He saw pushcarts with peddlers selling vegetables, fish, and apples. Kids pulled wagons, sat with dogs on fire escapes, and sold shopping bags. Signs on painted buildings decreed, "Children Cry for Castoria," "Time to take Hood's Sarsaparilla," "Madame Butterfly Cigars," and "Ex-lax." In some areas, the signs were in Yiddish. Other sections of their ride passed over hills and through vistas of green parks only to turn past more tenement buildings.

Over and over, the train screeched to a stop, the conductor pulled the chain, the bell rang "ting, ting," and the train jerked to a start again. Ezra became more and more nervous. They traveled from Brooklyn across Manhattan and into the Bronx. Just when he thought the trip would never end, the El stopped, and his father said, "Well, this is it."

Mr. Katz showed the address on his paper to a few people. "Yes, very Jewish name," they said and pointed to an old, drab brownstone structure. Ezra was disappointed when they entered the dark musty-smelling building, and his father sighed. They'd expected something finer.

A little girl in braids answered their knock at the apartment door.

"Is the rabbi home?" his father asked.

"Yes. Come in."

Ezra looked at the short man with a gray mustache and a Van-dyke beard. The rabbi wore a shiny silk coat dusted with cigarette ash over a fancy embroidered silk vest with a yarmulke on his head and a gold watch and chain hanging above his potbelly. Ezra felt sick.

The rabbi sat and gestured for them to sit. "Yes?" he said.

Mr. Katz's voice shook, and he started to cry while he unburdened himself to the rabbi, recounting how a matchmaker brought him and Gussie together as young immigrants into a loveless marriage. The rabbi listened and nodded at a familiar story, but the news stunned Ezra.

Mr. Katz switched to Ezra's crying spells. "My son has a nervous stomach. He cries and cries and cries. If he wants something, we give it to him. Still he cries. He won't tell us what he's crying about." Ezra broke out in sweat. What if the rabbi asked what he was crying about? He couldn't explain his recurring sadness.

But the rabbi just said, "Will you both please stand?" He prayed, swaying softly back and forth. The room spun and darkened around Ezra until he fainted on the floor. When he came to, he was sitting in the rabbi's chair with his feet on the footstool. "How do you feel, my boy?" the rabbi asked.

His father said, "The poor kid's fainted. He wouldn't touch a bite of food this morning. He was so anxious."

The rabbi promised to pray for Ezra at the synagogue every day and urged Ezra's family to pray for him. He said they should anoint his head with oil three times for three nights. Mr. Katz paid the rabbi's fee, and they walked down the steps in silence.

His father tried to make conversation going home with all the scenery there in reverse, but Ezra was no longer interested. His thoughts wrapped around the oil they would put on his head. Three times for three nights, his father rubbed Ezra's head with oil from a big tin can with gold lettering and said a prayer. They waited.

The sorrow returned to Ezra, followed by another crying spell. They did not go back to the Good Jew for a refund, figuring God must not have heard him that day. His mother did the only thing she knew to do. She made more orange Jell-O and topped it with whipped cream.

Another chronic worry for Benjamin and Gussie was Ezra's obsession with art as he returned to his painting. They could see his talent growing, but they worried. If he didn't find another interest, how would he make a living?

His parents' worry could not deter him. Ezra knew he had to create art, and he painted with whatever supplies he could find—a smooth piece of wood lying on a cellar door, discarded house paints, and burlap bags draped over the ends of wooden orange crates. A neighborhood house painter admired his work and became a friend. The painter had been beaten up by strikers, leaving him with a scar right across his forehead, but he welcomed Ezra as an equal into his hot apartment, where he sat in his undershirt and told the story of a guy who picked up a chair and broke his head open. He gave Ezra leftover house paints and tubes of color to mix with white to get the shades he wanted. Ezra diluted the potent sticky paint with mineral oil, and even though it left brown stains when the oil dried, he appreciated his benefactor and the paint.

Sometimes Ezra copied pictures from magazines of places he'd never been and people he'd never seen. He made a painting of a guy with a seaman's raincoat at a pilot's wheel using a pen to make multitudes of tiny dots. He painted gloomy scenes with graveyards and storms. Most often, Ezra used his eyes for ideas. He saw his father stretched across the bed asleep after working all night. Ezra noticed his father's backside and the soles of his feet. He saw ceilings and walls with flaking white paint. Outside, Ezra watched the laundry waving in the wind. He saw blue sun-shiny skies, and small clouds drifting across—things he could paint into a picture. A man across from Ezra's family used a big stick to train pigeons to fly in a big circle. They fluttered over the rooftops from his house to the Katz's house and back again. Ezra put the birds into his paintings.

Sometimes his mother would wake him at dawn. "Ezra, open your eyes just for a minute," she would say. "Look out the window."

He would see the red dawn as the sunrise colored the sky. "What colors!" she said. "Now, go back to sleep. Go back—," but he was already asleep.

Sometimes Ezra's found supplies didn't work well. He drew a picture of black storm clouds drifting by a lighthouse with waves crashing against it, but drops of the black paint oozed down from the clouds into the sea.

"I don't know how to stop it!" Ezra cried. "I'm no good. I quit."

"Hold it," his mother called. "I'll be right there!"

His mother hurried to the closet and poked through the fold-ing chairs, pots, tools, and junk until she found the painting she wanted. She showed Ezra the picture of a three-masted ship head-ing across the green sea with its sails billowing high into the sky. "Tell me who painted this," she said. Ezra looked at the picture.

He remembered copying it from a calendar cover, painting on burlap with the house paint and a few tubes of color his friend had given him. Using the picture as proof, Gussie reminded him that he was a good artist.

Ezra felt his mother's ambivalence toward him, and he returned the same. At times he saw the hard work she did and heard her wish she were a man so she could sail away in a boat, and he became empathetic. When he became discouraged with his art, she was the champion he needed, encouraging and urging him to continue, and he was grateful. On ordinary days, she was the mother who made Jewish chicken soup with everything in it, including his favorites—the chicken's feet, especially the pads, the gizzards, and the developing eggs. Other times, she contended that she nearly died at his birth and had never come back to full health after the experience left her with her heart problems and varicose veins, or she became the neighborhood martyr, "the angel," as she cared for his chronic sinusitis, stomach problems, and general sickliness, and left him feeling guilty.

Uncle Louie, a regular guest at the family gatherings, was an alcoholic and smoked Prince Albert tobacco in a corncob pipe. While he and Ezra were rivals for many things, Ezra admired his offbeat character. Uncle Louie discovered a one-eyed cat in an alley. He named the cat Mazik, meaning rascal, which made Ezra think the cat and Uncle Louie were a matched set.

Uncle Louie's cat scratched their family guests and hissed at them until Aunt Rosa laid down the law. Mazik could not be excused just because he caught the mice that were brave enough to venture out at night. Uncle Louie and Aunt Rosa yelled and screamed at each other about the cat for days. Aunt Rosa said Mazik had to go.

Uncle Louie said, "So tell me. How can I do it?"

"You found him!" she screamed. "You get rid of him!"

Uncle Louie schemed. He lured Mazik into a bag and tied it with strong string. He took a zigzag route from home so the cat wouldn't know how to find the way back. The cat squirmed in the bag all the way. Uncle Louie loosened the strings just a bit so it would take a long time for Mazik to escape and left the cat in an empty lot before making his way back home. When he arrived home, Mazik sat on the steps waiting for him. Uncle Louie cried for joy, and Mazik became the king of the household, ruling from the living room lounge.

Ezra thought Uncle Louie's rascally antics matched the cat. Sometimes he heated pennies on the stove until they were red hot. He'd pick them up with teaspoons, put them on the kitchen table, and invite some unsuspecting kid to help himself. As he stood back, he pretended surprise when the kid yelled in pain.

Other suspicions about his uncle caused Ezra to hurry and hide his matchstick collection when Uncle Louie visited. They competed to grab the burned-out sticks anytime someone struck a match. If Uncle Louie won, he cackled with laughter, showing his yellow teeth under a gray moustache. When Ezra used his collection to build castles, log cabins, and trains, he wondered what Uncle Louie did with his matchsticks.

One day after Uncle Louie left, Ezra wandered around the room touching this and that and happened to look in his match-book bag. All but one matchstick was gone. Ezra ran to Uncle Louie's house to confront him.

Aunt Rosa was sipping tea with some of her neighborhood friends. Uncle Louie sat in a rocker beside Mazik with his back to the guests.

He looked at Ezra. "What ya starin' at? See a circus, maybe?"

"My matchsticks are missing. Did you take them?"

"What? You say such things to an old man?"

"What do you need 'em for?" Ezra asked.

"Mind your business. Go play with the bums in the street."
He puffed on his pipe and blew smoke at Ezra. Ezra left gasping
for breath.

Ezra became jealous of Mazik's good life and special attention,
which seemed unfair since the only time he received any particular notice was when his mother admired his paintings. He got a
bright idea from a story he'd read in school about a boy who left
home to seek his fortune. The boy had grand adventures, whis-
tling a tune as he traveled along, carrying his stuff in a polka dot
handkerchief tied to the end of a stick slung over his shoulder.
Ezra packed his crayons, matchsticks, and a deck of cards in a
red dishtowel and tied it to the end of a stick.

"I'm running away from home," he said to his mother.

She got up from the floor she was scrubbing. "Okay. Your sack's
not tied right. Here, let me fix it." She retied his bundle and went
back to scrubbing the floor, perhaps to teach him not to run away
by pretending not to care.

Ezra strolled aimlessly down the street past the rickety ice
wagon with the mustachioed driver in a straw hat cracking his
whip and muttering, "Giddyap." He saw the woman in her kerchief in the little wooden candy stand selling wax false teeth,
licorice braids, and chocolate babies. A bunch of older guys in
a doorway stopped him and soon had his dishtowel opened on
the street. "Wow—a deck of cards!" A guy named Heshie jumped
down and snatched them. "Don't worry. You can watch. I'm gonna
give 'em back to you later. Don't worry." Ezra stopped to watch the
boys play, shuffling, dealing, and snapping cards. Finally, some
of them left, straggling home as they got hungry for supper.

Needing another player, the boys asked Ezra to fill in. When the game finally broke up, they returned his cards, and Ezra retied his bundle and continued his trek.

It was dark when Ezra realized he was in enemy territory on Wyona Street. He heard, "Guys! A Vermonter!"

Ezra surprised himself at how fast he could run. He fell and snapped his stick in two. Wyonas closed in as he grabbed his bundle and headed for Uncle Louie's. He dashed upstairs and pounded on the door.

"Look who's here," said Aunt Rosa. "How come you tore your knee-pants?"

"What's that you're carrying?" asked Uncle Louie.

"I'm running away from home, so I came here. Do you have a place for me to sleep?"

Aunt Rosa said, "Sure. You can sleep on the lounge."

Ezra looked over as Mazik glared at him, ruling from the lounge under a huge rubber plant fertilized with discarded tea leaves and tobacco ash.

"You'd like some milk maybe?" asked Aunt Rosa.

"Yeh, thanks. I always have a little cake and milk before I go to bed."

"We don't have no cake," said Uncle Louie. "How about a game of Casino?" Uncle Louie won every game as usual. Ezra suddenly began to worry about his matchsticks. As if Uncle Louie could read his mind, he pulled out his own big matchstick bag, carried it to the coal stove, lifted one of the stove lids, and emptied his stash into the fire. A huge flame rose up with great crackling. Uncle Louie stroked his mustache while Mazik's eye gleamed in the light as he meowed.

Now Ezra knew what Uncle Louie did with his matchsticks, and his heart broke thinking of all the log cabins and castles he could have built with them. "I think I better go home," he said.

Home might not be perfect, but Ezra began to see that it had advantages.

"Doncha' like it here?" asked Uncle Louie.

"I'm used to cake with my milk," said Ezra.

Aunt Rosa told him to be careful and to give her regards to the family. He grabbed his bundle and went out into the night. He'd never been out alone so late, and the streetlights looked strange in the dark.

As he neared home, he could see all the lights on. His mother's floor scrubbing had been because she expected company. Ezra looked at his bruised and dirty self and wondered how he would be received in such a special gathering. He could hear the party with people laughing and talking as he climbed the steps. He reached the door and peered through the beveled glass pane. The ceiling light was on with its many colors—amber, blue, and yellow. Caruso sang *Aida* from the Victrola. He heard the fizz as someone poured club soda and thought surely there must be some sponge cake, too.

He tried the door, but it was locked.

He knocked. Nothing.

He knocked harder.

"Who is it?" He could see his mother's shape, hazy behind the glass.

"It's me. Ezra. I'm back."

"No. You can't come in. You can't come back. You ran away from home."

Ezra kicked and banged on the door. He yanked on the doorknob and cried. He crawled along the floor looking for a way in. "Please, let me in. I'll be good. I won't run away again."

He heard his father. "Why don't you give him another chance?"

His mother discussed it with the guests. Finally, she opened the door. "Oy—*Gotenyu*! Look at him."

The lights hurt his eyes. Somebody washed his face, and they gave him cake and milk.

After that, he was good for a long time, observing all the amenities to get himself back in his mother's good graces. "Thank you." "Please." "Yes." "Excuse me." "May I?"

For many nights, he dreamed of being in the strange dark, trying to get home. Old women chased him with candles to light their way. In his dream, he couldn't scream or run fast enough to get away. The women came closer and closer. He woke up shaking and sweating just before they grabbed him. Sometimes his brother stretched his hand across the bed and asked, "You okay?" but then Kelly fell back asleep.

The crying spells finally stopped when he was about nine, but the art controversy continued as his talent grew and his reputation began to spread through the little community. A seaman neighbor, whom he hardly knew, came back from Holland bringing him a watercolor set. Ezra recognized its endless possibilities as he looked at the fresh clean squares of thirty colors, fifteen on each side, with three finger-shaped hollows for mixing colors. He held it by the two circular metallic strings on the bottom like a palette. Ezra painted until the colors wore down in the center and even until he had scraped all the bits of color from the edges.

In the meantime, his father observed artists in the neighborhood—strange, hungry, homeless people—hardly enough money for a cup of coffee at the rundown diner where he worked—not the life he wanted for Ezra. Still, both of his parents could see his love for art and his talent. In their ambivalence, they alternated between cheering him on and cajoling him into other activities.

His mother, as his encourager, might be his lookout as he painted in the afternoon after school. She'd listen for the downstairs door. "Quick," she'd say. "It's Pa. Put everything away. We'll talk later."

The painting, palette, paint box, brushes, and rags disappeared under the cover of the flowered oilcloth on the foot-pedaled Singer sewing machine. But his father would see Ezra washing his hands and catch the scent of turpentine and linseed oil.

"What do I smell? Do you want to starve like those Bohemians I see every day in the Village? You want to be another poor slob? Get out in the street and play ball like other kids."

Ezra scurried outside and left his parents arguing over what to do with him. None of them had any prescience that he would find stories on the street that would one day be companions to his art.

CHAPTER 3

LIFE ON VERMONT STREET

SUMMER WEATHER ON VERMONT STREET FOUND KIDS CON-structing adventures. Zoody followed the ice truck, watching for his opportunity. Catching the iceman with his back turned, he jumped on the back of the truck and shoved off a block of ice that shattered into sparkling shreds. Kids grabbed the ice and disappeared, watching from their hideouts until the iceman was gone and they could gather safely on the hot sidewalk to sit and eat their ice.

Boys shaved their heads for the hot weather. Even more impor-tant than keeping their heads cool, their "baldies" showed off any "scarfalife (scar for life)," a badge of importance, evidence of a previous injury. Those with several signifying accidents or previ-ous fights earned the most prestige. Zoody acquired a scarfalife and a broken leg when he jumped from the fire escape with an umbrella for a parachute. Duddie exhibited the best from time spent on a farm where he held the wood across a log to help the farmer chop timber. One day, the farmer's rhythm was off, and he chopped Duddie's forefinger off about halfway down. Duddie came back to the neighborhood with his finger in a black sling strapped around his waist. Ezra was horrified when Duddie took it off to show him an injury that would have done a man proud who had been in a sea battle.

Some boys gained a scarfalife riding in the neighborhood wagon, which the boys built by nailing a crate to a long plank of wood with a shorter board crosswise at the other end, adding carriage wheels and a rope for the driver. The route was nonstop from Vermont Street around the block to Wyona Street, where their rivals lay in wait. Street fights did not divide along racial or religious lines but on loyalty to one's own block, each block a microcosm of a country pulling together in the conflict.

One day, Ezra drove the wagon with Jackie for the pusher. The great ride ended in enemy territory, where they heard the shouts, "Vermonters! Get them!"

Wyonas came up from the curb, ran out of hallways, and yelled from the windows. A couple of boys punched and hit Ezra and Jackie, but Jackie held on and pushed the wagon hard over the cracked and broken pavement, back to Vermont Street and safety. The Vermonters put up an old bedspring in the alley as a shield between the two streets. They threw whatever they could pick up from the street, and the Wyonas fled. But the Wyonas were not really gone. They circled around in both directions and caught the Vermonters from behind. Both sides started shoving as curses and dire threats filled the air. Zoody, the Vermont Street leader, fought it out with the Wyona Street leader, pounding each other with bruised knuckles until they were too tired to fight anymore. Each gang walked off toward home with its captain, giving him comfort and checking to see if he had a new scarfalife.

Sometimes the kids played and fought in the schoolyard across the street from Ezra's house, with courageous kids scaling the cast-iron fence topped with tall spikes that surrounded the yard. If one of these brave souls impaled himself on the spikes, the others rescued him and took him to the pharmacist to patch him up. Sometimes an iron bar was mysteriously sawed out during the night, giving even the timid kids a chance to rush through and play until the fence was repaired.

Duddie and Ezra were at outs and not speaking one day, when a bully picked a fight with Ezra in the schoolyard. Ezra fought hard until he heard Duddie yell, "Come on, Ezra, hit him!" Surprised and happy that Duddie was cheering him on, he looked at Duddie for just a second. That second was long enough for the bully to send his fist crashing into Ezra's nose, fracturing his septum and giving his nose a small permanent tilt. Ezra had his own scarfalife.

Neighborhood mothers took care of all the children. If Ezra and a friend got sweaty and went into a house, both boys would get the same treatment from the friend's mother who would take off their hats, mop their brows, blow their noses, dry their hair, stick the hats back on, and send them both back to play in the street. Walls were thin, and the Katz family could hear neighbors partying or arguing. Summer days found the Vermonters on the street until evening came and mothers called.

"D-u-u-u-die!"

"H-e-e-e-e-shey!"

"Ayr-o-o-o-o-me! Don't make me spit out my lungs. I'm calling you!"

"M-o-o-o-ris! Come home arready. Wait'll I get my hands on you!"

Slowly the kids left the games and straggled home.

Winter brought a different kind of magic to Vermont Street. Ezra and his friends watched as snow fell softly and gently. Streets disappeared and everything took on white shapes. Teddy, who was older, bigger, and tougher, pulled Ezra on the sled and teamed up for the snowball fights, building the strongest snow fort on the block. Some of the boys made fun of Teddy's friendship with

Ezra. Why would he want to hang out with a skinny kid who was too scared to jump a ride on a trolley or dare to have other big adventures?

Teddy and his mother, abandoned by his father, lived above the Katz family. Teddy loved hanging around and enjoyed Mrs. Katz's cooking for most of his meals and even bragged that he and Ezra were really cousins. Saturdays, Teddy and Ezra went to the movies together. Between showings, they hid in the bathroom so they could see the movie again. For the next week, they entertained the other kids in the neighborhood with all the details of the movie.

One night a bully named Lefty and his gang stopped Teddy and Ezra. They were carrying what they called "Indian clubs." Americans, who had borrowed the idea of these exercise clubs from the British who had borrowed them from India, used them for health and bodybuilding. Lefty looked at Teddy, "You gonna hang around with this little sissy?"

Teddy said nothing, but Ezra saw sweat pop out over his face. Maybe Lefty and his gang planned to use the exercise clubs for something other than developing their muscles.

Lefty poked him in the stomach, "W-E-L-L?"

"Yeah." Teddy sounded hoarse.

Exercise clubs and arms began to swing. Teddy defended himself the best he could, but Ezra heard the clubs hitting Teddy's head until the gang finally grew tired and left. Ezra felt helpless during the fight and ashamed afterward, feeling like he deserved the skinny sissy description. Ezra helped Teddy wash up as he took off his shirt and soaked it in the fountain. They walked and talked until it was past time for Teddy's mother to be asleep— when he could go home without being questioned—their friendship closer than ever.

Ezra accidentally discovered two ways to outwit the bullies. He had become the unofficial artist of the block, using a stub of a pencil and a brown paper bag from the grocery or, on lucky days, a found piece of plain paper. One day he walked home with one of his paintings, a copy of Norman Rockwell's watchmaker from the *Saturday Evening Post*. He had taken it, as he often did when he was proud of his artwork, to show Mr. Gordon, the luncheonette owner, who he considered to be his number one fan. He met a gang of boys, and one of them ripped the painting out of his hands.

"Who done dis?"

Ezra figured the boy was going to put his fist through the painting. "I did."

"Ya did?"

Another boy spoke up. "He's kidding us."

"Nah," one of them said. "He musta done it. I seen him drawin' on paper bags."

"Geez," the first guy said. He handed the painting back. "So long, Doc." Doc became Ezra's nickname, and the bullies treated him with respect.

About this time, Ezra began telling stories. A mob of kids would surround him, including the neighborhood bullies, even their leader Lefty, a tough guy who would be killed in a gang fight at seventeen. Starting with an idea—possibly about a battleship and some sailors—he would add something exciting and dangerous: maybe they climbed a mast and were shot down. Kids followed him around the block begging him to tell them a story.

One night, Lefty and his gang beat up some other kids on the playground. When they came to Ezra, Lefty said, "Nah, let him go." At the time, Ezra's stories had made him special and bought him safety, but they were secondary to his paintings, and he did not envision how storytelling would one day become a companion to his art.

Sometimes Ezra became the trickster. All the kids saved stamps. They sent away for catalogs of stamps from faraway places. Ezra copied a postage stamp from his collection into his homework book, but he decided it looked pretty dull. He began to create his own stamps in many shapes—long rectangles, triangles, ovals—and added giraffes, tigers, palm trees, and other exotic scenes. He took his sister's manicure scissors and cut tiny serrated notches around the edges. As a final touch, he copied cancellation marks and smeared them with his dirty fingers. Since the stamps looked real to him, he wondered if they could fool somebody else.

Bubbie, the stamp expert, had the best collection in the neighborhood. Ezra invited him into the dimly lit hallway of the tenement to show off his designs, saying they might blow away outside. He spread his creations on the floor.

"Wow! Where'd you get them?" asked Bubbie.

Ezra thought quickly. "A sailor. My cousin. He came back from a trip around the world and brought them to me."

"Want to swap?" Bubbie looked hopeful.

Ezra bargained with him and traded two of his counterfeits for four or five of Bubbie's best stamps. Bubbie wanted more, but Ezra said, "I want to keep the rest. I might get a better deal." Bubbie's hands shook as he put his new treasures into his album. He headed out to the street, and Ezra went inside to peek out from behind the curtain.

Outside in the daylight, Bubbie realized he'd been tricked. He ran back up the steps, yelling all the way. He banged on Ezra's door and pronounced curses on him, his father, his mother, his sister, and his brother. "I'll make you eat them in front of all the guys," he said.

Through the bolted door, Ezra suggested a peace talk, but Bubbie banged and yelled louder. Ezra shook violently. Finally, he slipped Bubbie's rare stamps under the door. Bubbie ran down the steps, still pronouncing curses on Ezra's family. Ezra watched out the window until Bubbie disappeared around the corner. He waited until much later before he ventured out. When he opened his door, there were his beautiful counterfeits shredded into tiny bits.

Kids weren't the only ones who made life challenging for Ezra. One day the boys screamed and yelled as they chased each other over fire hydrants, around garbage cans, and over cellar doors. Suddenly, one of the doors flew open. Out sprang a red-haired, dust-covered giant. "Why can't you leave me alone? I want to pray! I want some quiet!"

It was the zaddik, or holy person. The boys already thought he was strange because he could carry huge sacks of coal or big chunks of ice—even a secondhand upright piano. He accepted little pay for his work, just enough to get by. He spent his days in prayer, but now he was angry and loud. Ezra didn't wait to see what the other boys did but ran headlong until he reached home and burst into the room with his mother and Kelly. "That zaddik chased me! He's after me."

Although Ezra thought his brother looked scared, Kelly said, "I'll go talk to him." Like a typical big brother, Kelly gave Ezra a hard time at home but took care of him with ominous outsiders or bullies. After a while, Kelly came back and seemed different as he spoke softly. "The zaddik is a good man. He'll never hurt you. Don't be afraid of him."

When Ezra gained enough courage to pass the zaddik's place again, he found a smooth piece of wood lying on his cellar door. Had the zaddik left it there for him? Ezra took the board home and decided it was time to use his few colors of real artist paint, bought with his saved-up spending money. He squeezed out blue and white and mixed them carefully. He covered his board with blue. He dipped his brush in the white paint, squiggled it on the board, and let it trail off. It became a little cloud floating across a blue sky. Ezra was amazed. For the rest of his life, every time he saw a tiny cloud floating across the sky, he remembered this day and his painting on the zaddik's board.

Nobody in his neighborhood seemed to know where or how to get real art materials, so Ezra took that problem to his brother. Kelly said, "Why don't you write to Clara Bow? She's a Brooklyn girl. Tell her you like to draw and would like a painting set, that you are a kid from Brooklyn and one of her fans. It'll be a great publicity stunt for her." Ezra wrote his request with care on nice lined paper, sent it to Hollywood, and waited. In about a month, he received a glossy, autographed picture of the "It" girl, but he remained unclear as to what "It" was.

In his next effort, Ezra wrote to "Daddy" Browning, the millionaire who had married the young "Peaches," who would later star in the Peaches Browning case, a tabloid scandal involving Daddy Browning's marriage to the sixteen-year-old at fifty-two and the possibility that he had arranged an acid attack on her face. Knowing Daddy Browning's reputation for generosity to children at Christmastime, Ezra requested a painting set. He didn't receive an answer, not even a glossy of "Peaches." Realizing he was on his own, Ezra continued painting with found items, with muslin stretched over ends of orange crates, and with scrounged house paints.

Christmastime came and Mrs. Kraus, Ezra's Ukrainian neighbor on the second floor, invited him up to see their Christmas tree. He walked into a dark room and saw a tree with tiny lights going off and on. Mrs. Kraus gave him Christmas foods to take back and share with his family. The Katz family enjoyed the neighborly gesture and a few months later at Passover, his mother thought she would return this favor with her Jewish holiday food and made a nice package including nuts, raisins, and matzos. Mrs. Katz took pride in her special dishes, expecting them to be received with pleasure. Mrs. Kraus told Ezra's mother later that her husband made her throw them all away.

Young Ezra puzzled over this rejection and stored the hurt in his mind. He enjoyed the rich traditions around him, brought from many countries, and thought they added variety to his life. As he checked out the different churches and synagogues in his neighborhood, he peeked into one church and saw colored glass windows and a statue of a woman with a shawl over her head holding a baby, tenderly and sadly. He especially liked to linger around the one Duddie's family attended, the New Mission Storefront Church. He heard sweet sadness in the songs that drifted out into the street: "Go Down, Moses" and "We're in the Same Boat, Brother." He thought the variety in his neighborhood was something to celebrate. Why wouldn't Mr. Kraus want his family to enjoy their special holiday foods? It was yet another quandary he would save to consider.

Anticipation filled the neighborhood air when Charles Lindbergh took off in his plane, the *Spirit of St. Louis*, from Roosevelt Field on Long Island on 20 May 1927. Could he make it all the way across the Atlantic? The newfangled radio gave hourly bulletins to keep everybody informed. In a Yankee Stadium boxing match, the announcer paused to relay Lindbergh's latest position. The forty thousand spectators rose for a minute of silent prayer for the pilot's safety. In Brooklyn, Ezra and his friends joined the excitement. Tuned in to the radio, they listened for reports on sightings of the plane. The news came on 21 May: the aviator landed in Paris—thirty-three hours and thirty minutes after his takeoff. America had a new hero, known as "Lucky Lindy."

With other Americans, Ezra and his friends waited for Lindbergh to finish the celebrations in Paris. They waited again after he landed in Washington, DC, for another parade and reception. Finally, on Monday, 13 June 1927, he flew to Long Island and transferred to an amphibious plane that took him to the city yacht. He sailed up the harbor to the Battery in southern Manhattan, surrounded by five hundred ships of various shapes and sizes. An estimated four and a half million people lined the streets for the ticker-tape parade through Manhattan. Three hundred thousand people, including New York governor Alfred E. Smith, greeted him in Central Park. The Vermont Street boys followed it all on the radio, waiting for their turn with the great conqueror.

Knowing a Brooklyn parade would come next, Ezra got ready. He cut out a picture of Lindy and stuck it in the window. He hung out little American flags. Ezra kept checking for parade sounds. Since nearby Sutter was such a big avenue, surely the parade would have to come. He ran out every time he heard a noise and looked to the left down Sutter Avenue, figuring the parade must be coming. He waited and waited. Weeks later, the signs were still in the streets, Ezra's picture and flags were still in his window, but Lucky Lindy never came to his neighborhood. Even a great hero might let you down. What was a kid to do?

The following year, Ezra listened to the presidential election speeches and heard Governor Al Smith using his identification with immigrants and common people in his campaign. In a world that never seemed quite right, maybe there was something Ezra could do. He decided to write a letter and a poem for his favorite candidate. He would sign it officially with his school signature.

438 Vermont Street
Brooklyn, NY
October 8, 1928

My dear Governor Al Smith

I am taking great pleasure in writing you, and trust that you will spare a few moments in reading a little poem I wrote and composed myself and hope you are pleased with it.

To Al
Vote for Smith antidry
He'll be president by and [by]
Down with the dry
Up with the wet
Roosevelt will be governor of
New York yet.
Vote for Smith he's a real
    New Yorker
Oh, Boy! He sure is a
Corker
Of Thomas, Ottinger Hoover
And all the rest
I think Smith is the best
Vote for Smith anti dry
He'll be president by and by

He closed the letter with "I am your little patriot, Sincerely, Jack E Katz."

Governor Smith lost the election in a landslide to Herbert Hoover.

CHAPTER 4

*H*ARD *C*HANGES AND *O*PPORTUNITIES

IN ANOTHER STEP DOWN IN THE WORLD, EZRA'S FAMILY HAD moved from the railroad flat into a tenement house before he entered junior high in PS #149 in 1929. Danny Kaye, renowned entertainer who had attended PS #149, recorded a school song about it:

> 149 is the school for me,
> Drives away all adversity,
> Steady and true we will be to you.

In Ezra's own observation, adversity, instead of being driven away, only showed up in new forms. Ezra overheard the school principal, as she stood looking out the window, "I'm the principal of the school, and I don't have a car and yet the Jews in the neighborhood have one." This puzzling statement made no sense to Ezra. Anytime there was a car on his street, somebody was sick and had sent for the doctor, who only had a little Model T Ford. Poverty followed these students like a stray dog looking for a home. How could Miss Richardson come to such a conclusion?

Mr. Katz bought an elaborate cake decorated with roses and other flowers for Ezra to take to the school faculty to atone for the trouble caused by his chronic absences with fevers, sinusitis, and bloody noses.

The principal asked, "Did your mother make this?"

"No," he said. "It was bought."

Since the cake was purchased, she said, "Okay," and accepted the gift. She would have refused anything one of the Jewish women baked for fear of some kind of contamination, with her prejudice becoming her own loss, since Mrs. Katz was an excellent cook.

Even Ezra's Bar Mitzvah turned out to be disappointing. His parents and a few neighbors gathered for the celebration when he came home for lunch one day. They said prayers, ate a few raisins and nuts, gave him a tie for a present, and sent him back to school. He'd expected it to be held in a fancier place with high cushions and music to go with the prayers, with some kind of magic—something better than the same old tenement.

But there were bright spots mingled with the adversity, beginning with his mother, who could attend parent conferences and make herself understood because she spoke without the heavy accent of many of his friends' parents.

His brother had a friend named Louie who took an interest in him. Louie lived in a sparsely furnished apartment with his mother, a revolutionary Russian who had escaped by the skin of her teeth. Unlike other people who were older than him, Louie talked to Ezra like a real person. He introduced him to Darwin's *Origin of the Species.* Most of the book baffled him, but he became enchanted with evolution and began drawing dinosaurs. Louie shared his own drawings with Ezra and read poetry to him, quoting Shelley and Keats in casual conversation.

The best thing that happened to Ezra came when he failed algebra, necessitating his attendance at summer school, where he met a new friend nicknamed "Itz" or "Itch," short for Isadore. Ezra was almost two years older than Itch but in the same grade because of the time he had lost in school with all his illnesses. Itch knew his algebra but had sassed the teacher, and summer school became his punishment.

The boys lived less than two blocks from each other in a community struggling to eke out a living, Itch on the fourth floor and Ezra on the third floor of walk-up tenements where their mothers stretched every dollar. Their mothers made clothes from remnants of cloth and soup from bones, delicious potato soup that filled their stomachs along with homemade bread that was both cheaper and better than bread from the store. Itch's mother made his undershirts from soft cotton flour sacks, leaving him with the impression that all undershirts came with the symbol of a brand of flour on the front. In the community, borrowing and lending kitchen utensils became a way of life. Mrs. Katz might say, "Mrs. Blatt, may I borrow your potato masher?" Though they had been friends for many years, they still addressed each other formally.

Enjoying their new friendship, Ezra and Itch played handball before and after classes and drank Mrs. Katz's lemonade. She made it with real lemons, rinds and all, put slivers of ice in it, and kept it in the icebox. On those hot summer days without air-conditioning, her lemonade seemed like the coldest thing in the universe. Itch thought it was amazing, and they drank every drop. Mrs. Katz said, "I don't mind, but I can't believe you drank it all."

They read and discussed the same books, retelling the stories to each other and passing them around from hand to hand with their other friends since actual ownership was expensive. Favorites included books written for their age group, including the Horatio Alger rags-to-riches books, *Tarzan of the Apes*, Tom Swift's inventions, and Nick Carter detective stories. They also read classics: the works of Rudyard Kipling, Jack London, Mark

Twain, and O. Henry. At the movies, they laughed at Charlie Chaplin, Buster Keaton, and Our Gang; experienced adventure with Douglas Fairbanks, Tom Mix, and Bill Boyd; predicted the outcome of the weekly episode of the Westerns; and experienced the thrill of Dracula and Frankenstein. By the end of the summer, Ezra and Itch were friends for life.

As if they were not poor enough already, news came on 29 October 1929 that the stock market had crashed. None of these immigrant families had investments, but they were among the first to lose their jobs in the Great Depression. Boys like Ezra and Itch looked for ways to work and help their families with the groceries or to earn a nickel for the Saturday matinee.

Itch worked for the pharmacist, running errands and cleaning up. Once he was on a ladder putting chemicals in order on the top shelves. Just as he reached to put the nitroglycerine away, it slipped and fell. With movie knowledge of the explosive qualities of the product, Itch's life passed before him. However, it hit the floor with an ordinary thud, and Itch survived to fulfill his destiny as a distinguished professor of chemistry.

The pharmacist took care of most of the community medical problems. They called him "Dr." Berliner, and Ezra considered him an ally. Dr. Berliner spoke out about the awful taste of cod liver oil and the feeling it left of shrinking into a prune. When people came in for wonder cures, the pharmacist would say, "Do you really need it? It doesn't do any good, you know. Why don't you take an aspirin?" He'd suggest a morning round of hot water with lemon or tea and honey. Emboldened by the pharmacist's derogatory remarks about folk cures and patent medicines, Ezra poured his cod liver oil down the sink and stuck his pills in his pocket when no one was looking.

Ezra also liked hanging around the pharmacy because of all the things to see and hear. If a kid came in who was hurt in a street fight, Dr. Berliner took him in the back, where he kept a first aid kit and a cot and sometimes gave Ezra the honored assignment of holding the gauze or iodine. Only if stitches were needed did Dr. Berliner call an ambulance.

Ezra's brother Kelly trained in a Western Union program that allowed boys to work in the daytime. By law, the employer had to ensure that the boys went to what was called a continuation school at night after they spent their days delivering telegrams. Neighbors shook with fear when they saw the uniformed messengers, knowing they seldom brought good news. The messages were often followed by screams and fainting, but with good tips, the messenger boys might earn ten dollars a week (one hundred dollars at today's value).

On Kelly's graduation night, Mr. Katz put on a shirt and tie, and Mrs. Katz wore her black dress and fake pearls. Mae and Ezra dressed in their finest clothes. The family, in the front row of the balcony, waited nervously. Kelly delivered his valedictory in a clear, gentle voice. Mr. Katz admired his son in his uniform of riding breeches, cap, visor, and highly polished shoes. "Look at him," he said. "A regular general. He looks like a regular general."

Ezra found his own moneymaking opportunities to help his family, some more successful than others. On Coney Island Beach, kids would go to a store a couple of blocks away and get a box of sodas and ice cream to peddle. They walked along hawking their wares to sunbathers who were loath to leave their towels. Families having picnics, people buried in the sand, and couples on blankets found the service quite convenient. When all their goods were sold, the young entrepreneurs returned the money to the store and received a share of the profits.

Tax-paying concessionaires, who sold food down on the beach, made sure policemen rounded up kids who hurt their sales with these catered snacks. When the storeowners who provided the wares were questioned, they explained, "I never tell the kids to go to the beach."

Customers who saw a policeman coming would call, "Hide!" The young peddler would drop his box, and somebody would cover it with a blanket as he sat down, making him a new family member. Other times, he might try to outrun the policeman, weaving in and out through the crowd of people. The fine was five dollars if he was caught, more than he could earn in months of peddling.

Ezra formed a plan in case he was ever trapped, thinking back to a former job working a pushcart for a food market, when the man from Sheffield Street who rented out the carts would ask, "You want a pushky?" If he was ever arrested, his name would become Joseph Pushky, and he would live on Sheffield Street.

Armed with a plan and a box of snacks, Ezra crossed under the shadow of the boardwalk and stepped off into the sand. From behind the second pillar of the boardwalk, a policeman grabbed him. "You're on the beach. Whattaya doin'?"

Ezra trembled.

The policeman repeated, "Whattaya doin'? Are you selling soda? What's your name?"

"Joe-joe-joe-joseph Pushky."

"Spell it."

Ezra spelled it. The policeman said, "Where do you live?"

"349 Sheffield Street."

The policeman said, "How do you spell Sheffield?"

Ezra panicked. Did Sheffield have one "f" or two? He mumbled something through his chattering teeth while the policeman wrote it all down. "You gotta—you better go back, or you'll be in real trouble, because if I catch you, it's gonna' be serious."

Ezra's Coney Island career was over, and he looked for other jobs. He worked for Mr. Goldman, a watermelon dealer one summer. He went into the cellar by candlelight to load the water-melon cart and tossed the rats that had been caught by the traps into the sewer. When he finished, it was daylight, and he went home for breakfast before going back to work. He worked every day except the Saturday Sabbath. His salary of a dollar a day helped feed his family and gave him some respect as a wage earner. He enhanced his own wages by pilfering a dime a day when his boss went to lunch. The dime, burning a hole in his pocket, brought fear that Mr. Goldman's prizefighting son would catch him and beat him up, but his need for art supplies out-weighed both his conscience and the danger. He bought crayons and cardboard that was black on one side and white on the other and enjoyed experimenting with light colors against the black. At the end of the week, Mr. Goldman gave him a big hunk of watermelon to split with his family. He relished the status that his dollar-a-day earnings gave him among his family even more that the juicy sweetness of the shared melon. Because he was now a breadwinner, his family listened to and valued his opinions at the supper table.

Ezra often took his paintings to show Mr. Gordon in the lun-cheonette when he went to buy ice cream. Mr. Gordon would say, "Tck, tck, tck. Look at what this kid did." One day, Mr. Gor-don gave Ezra a job. Mr. Gordon was going to be an agent for the Kodak film company, sending out film for developing and printing, and he asked Ezra to paint a huge sign for his window with all the information.

Ezra took a long sheet of wrapping paper and all his paint supplies. Using multiple colors and every type of lettering he had ever seen, he made every word, every letter different, adding decorations and exclamations marks. People would know what a bargain they were getting from his sign that said,

Kodak Film Developed and Printed Here!
Quick Service—One Week. 20 ¢

Neighborhood kids heard that Ezra had a real job, not just two cents for running errands, and they gathered to accompany him when he delivered the sign. Mr. Gordon hung the sign in his window and came outside to inspect it. He reached into his apron pocket and took out two shiny quarters and handed them to Ezra. Ezra grinned while his friends gasped. Nobody was ever paid that much money.

Mr. Katz went to the store to see the sign. Standing with his hands in his pockets and a big grin on his face, he thought maybe his son could become a sign painter, and maybe he would not starve. Mr. Katz told Ezra, "You did a beauty of a job for Mr. Gordon. Did it occur to you that you could own your own painting shop? Be your own boss? Have your name on the window? Not to worry about asking for jobs, hat in hand. You understand, don't you?"

"Yeah," Ezra said, but he wasn't excited about a life of painting signs.

A few days later, his father came home after working all night to find Ezra eating breakfast.

"How's the sign painting business?" he asked.

Ezra mumbled sleepily over his cocoa, "Nothing new."

"Wait'll you hear this," Mr. Katz said. "My boss wants you to paint a sign for the restaurant." He pulled out a crumpled piece of paper and read aloud.

New low prices at Pete's Coffee Pot!
Two Eggs with Potatoes and Coffee—10 ¢
Pigs Feet and Sauerkraut—25 ¢
Pancakes and Sausage—

His mother interrupted. "Hurry up with breakfast, Ezra. You're already late for school. Ben, why don't you talk about it when he gets back and finishes his homework?" Ezra left them arguing and headed for school.

Ezra worked on the sign for his father's boss in the evenings, taking extra care with the strange foods and even stranger spellings.

Mr. Katz came home one morning and saw the finished sign. "Beautiful! They never had such a fancy sign. You know what? Bigger and better jobs are coming. I can guarantee it." Since Mr. Katz had asked his boss for one dollar for the new sign, he pointed out that Ezra's pay had doubled.

After school, his father took a long walk with Ezra, talking man-to-man with him as they strolled. Ezra felt like an equal and thought everybody must be watching him, walking and talking with his father. The experience felt like floating along the sidewalk.

His father, having decided the money should go for sign paint-er's brushes, took Ezra the next Saturday to shop in Greenwich Village for art supplies, in the section of New York where actors, musicians, and artists lived. They stopped first to get Ezra's pay at the rundown diner, where a rusting tin coffeepot cutout with the owner's signature swung in front of Pete's Coffee Pot. The counterman said Pete was sorry not to be there, but he gave Ezra his dollar and treated them to jelly donuts and coffee. As they left, they paused in front of Ezra's sign. Mr. Katz said, "Next stop—real sign painting stuff."

Ezra followed his habit of observation as they walked through Greenwich Village. Tilted two- and three-story houses shared space with musty used bookstores and shops with their signs: Books Bought, Rare Books, Back Number Magazines, Prints, and

Art Reproductions. Right between a foreign film movie house and a pawnshop, they found the art supply store.

Ezra's eyes could hardly take in what he saw as they entered. Stacks of drawing paper in different colors, textures, and thicknesses stretched across the floor. Around the walls were canvas rolls, other canvases already stretched tight waiting for paint, and small fragile easels that shared space with fancy ones of expensive wood with cranks for raising, lowering, and tilting. And then he saw the paints—Naples yellow, cerulean blue, chrome orange, emerald green, mars red—row after row of colors in glass cases and on the counters. Fat tubes. Skinny tubes. Labels of Coleurs Extra Fins, Bellini, Pellican, Ölfarben Für Künstler. There seemed to be no end. His mind whirled.

Finally, they came to the brushes. Ezra's father said, "Now, what brushes do you need?" An overwhelmed Ezra took a deep breath, but nothing came out.

"Wake up," his father said. "We finally found them." Pooling their money, they bought three brushes and some tubes of paint.

"Now you are a professional," said Mr. Katz.

On the way out of the store, they passed two little old men in battered hats and threadbare baggy pants holding tubes of paint and whispering to each other. "Look, Pa," said Ezra. "That's Raphael Soyer and one of his brothers—Isaac or Moses."

Mr. Katz looked hard. "Who?"

"Raphael Soyer and one of his brothers. They're famous artists."

Mr. Katz looked again. Up and down. "That's famous?" he said.

Mr. Katz and Ezra took the El home. Ezra watched the city's shadows over pushcarts, the crowded streets, the shops, open windows with women and dogs peering out, and the endless signs until a couple boarded at one of the stops. Mr. Katz noticed and nudged him. The man, with hair that appeared not to have been combed in days, wore a red-checked shirt under a rumpled corduroy coat. The woman wore a long colorful skirt with a loose purple blouse and multiple strings of beads. His father elbowed Ezra. "See them? He's an artist, and she's his girlfriend or model. Maybe both."

Ezra, embarrassed that his father was talking too loud, whispered, "No, he's not. Why do you say that?"

"Where are your eyes? In the back of your head? Look in his right pocket."

Ezra saw a half dozen worn paintbrushes poking out of the man's jacket pocket. His eyes traveled down to the man's trousers and on to his paint-speckled shoes. His father folded his arms and heaved a self-satisfied sigh. They rode the rest of the way in silence.

At home, Ezra opened a tube of paint, looked at the color, and screwed the top back on. He lined the paint tubes up—gleaming yellow, rich velvety brown, elegant blue, and the blackest black. He arranged the brushes this way and that. Looking up at the window, he was startled to see the reflection of a real artist.

To get away from his troubles, Ezra often hid away and drew pictures or took long walks—anywhere to escape. On one of these walks, he found a treasure quite by accident. He detoured through the part of town in the upper class of poverty, where his classmate Harriet stood on the sagging porch of her family's unpainted house. When she returned Ezra's wave, his legs shuddered. Reassuring himself that he had not taken this route just to see Harriet, he traveled on—faster and faster.

Block after block, he moved into a new neighborhood, passing huge homes with green lawns, trimmed shrubs, and ancient trees. He looked over the white fences through the windows into very quiet houses and saw a world that seemed untroubled. Didn't these people have to go to work or shopping? Ezra had walked a little more than a mile, so far that he found himself in front of a different kind of building with tall pillars, huge doors, and rows of red brick steps. The sign said, "Brooklyn Public Library, Arlington Branch."

Ezra watched from the shade of a tree as smiling and chatting people went in and out. Following them inside, he smelled an unfamiliar aroma, the smell of books. In front of the rows and rows of bookshelves, people sat at tables and read from strange newspapers. Ezra looked around at the signs: Science. Politics. History. Fiction. Poetry. He took some stairs, with a riser labeled "Reference Room," to the loft. Right in front of him, he saw "Art." He pulled out a book about Egyptian art. He didn't understand all the words, but the book was fascinating. And the pictures. Artist Ezra felt important. There were more books on art—Greek, Italian, Chinese, Japanese—they went on and on. He discovered he could get a card and become a member of the library. He could take books home for free. Of course, he shared his find with Itch, and they began regular library excursions. Itch didn't go to the art area but turned to the science section when they arrived at the library. Ezra read every book on art, and Itch read every book on science.

As Ezra and Itch returned home from the library, Ezra pointed out the various shades of color in the autumn leaves followed by Itch's explanation that they had been there all along but were camouflaged by the green chlorophyll. When chlorophyll production stopped in the fall, the underlying colors came out. They talked about politics and world happenings, but their conversation was not finished when they got to Ezra's house, so Ezra walked Itch home. Back and forth, they walked each other home several times before one of them actually went inside.

Ezra practiced at home what he had seen in the art books. He carved from soap and wood and painted with anything he could find—even red mercurochrome. He assumed he'd found the newest thing in art, impressionism, since the art books ended with that period. He gathered the neighborhood artists and taught them to paint with little strokes of color, one next to the other. "Step back and they will all blend together in more vibrant colors," he told them. They were awed by his fancy word "vibrant," and soon all his friends were "Impressionists." They didn't know the movement was fifty years old and had already been replaced by other schools in developing movements of modern art. The library had run out of money to add updated books to its collection.

Mr. Katz called Ezra into the kitchen one day. "See this," he said. "A starving artist traded it for a bowl of soup. It's a good thing the boss wasn't around." He threw a brand-new tube of oil paint on the table. For several months, Mr. Katz brought home tubes in different colors traded for bowls of soup, always with the dire explanation that it was a deal with a starving artist. The deals he made added to Ezra's supply, but Ezra couldn't make himself use them. He kept thinking about the famished artists who had traded their paints for food. If Ezra had been suspicious, he might have realized that a new tube of paint cost more than a bowl of soup.

As the Depression became worse, Ezra caught on to something. Mr. Katz came in one morning, tired from his night's work. He brought Ezra a piece of cardboard with five small brushes on it, another trade from a starving artist. Ezra remembered seeing them in Woolworth's five-and-ten-cent store. They were cheap watercolor brushes for kids. Soon all the bristles would fall out. He turned the card over, and there was the price still on it. Ezra never let on that he'd discovered his father's secret. His father, who dreaded his future but had been buying the expensive paints all along, now had to take his business to the five-and-ten-cent store.

By this time, Ezra's father and other men were often hired for a job only to lose it again, making it difficult or impossible to pay the bills. Ezra was sent to do the family errands before he did his homework, and shopkeepers, who allowed people to buy on credit, heaped their abuse on him: "We know your father still ain't working. You tell your parents I'm a poor man, too. We ain't giving this food away free. A few more days and no more credit. Understand?" An embarrassed Ezra bought only the absolute requirements for existence before he scurried home and repeated the warnings to his family. He dreaded his return to the grocer, who would give him another lecture along with the bare necessities.

On his lunch hour, Ezra often had to pick up a bag of relief food given by the government to those in need. How Ezra hated this chore. The bags, stamped with a huge eagle and N. R. A. for National Recovery Administration, advertised that he was poor and taking government handouts. He believed his family sent him on these errands because he was the youngest and had the least status to lose.

As he started home with the bag one day, he saw Harriet, the belle of the school, headed right toward him. She hadn't seen him and his gaudy bag yet. Ezra couldn't give up his role as the dashing artist admired by Harriet with the fluttering eyelashes and the gray-blue eyes. The street was crowded, so he hurried into the first doorway, squeezed himself against the wall, and watched her go by.

His concealment made him late getting back to sell watermelons. Mr. Gordon yelled, "Where ya been? How can a man run a business when his help walks out on him? I oughtta dock ya for it."

Luckily, a customer came in, and Mr. Gordon turned. His voice became syrupy. "Halloo, Mrs. Berg. Cut a nice slice for Mrs. Berg to try. Just take a look at these melons—could make your mouth water—right, Mrs. Berg?"

With the family trapped in a bad situation with little hope of better days, Mrs. Katz gathered the three children one day and showed them three or four slices of white bread. "I want to explain something to you kids, so you won't misunderstand when you get hungry," she said. "This is all there is, this is all we have, and we just have to figure out how to make it last. And when there isn't any more, be prepared."

The community shared their trap. Out in the streets at night, Ezra heard political dissenters making speeches. A socialist might set up a stand and unroll a banner in front of his ladder. With a band and a torch to attract attention, a crowd formed quickly, and he would start shouting. Yelling across from him might be a Marxist who had read books about the revolution. They gave solutions for poverty and promoted equality for all people. Into this mix, Ezra saw a thirteen-year-old begin to argue, giving times and dates when proponents of each of their heroes ran amok or abandoned their cause, silencing all the opposition. When it was all over, Ezra cornered him to find out how he knew all this information. The boy said, "I made it up."

CHAPTER 5

REFUGE IN HIGH SCHOOL

AS EZRA ENTERED JEFFERSON HIGH SCHOOL, QUESTIONS OF what to do with his life loomed large. Mr. Katz couldn't make up his mind whether to encourage or discourage Ezra's art. All the artists he knew were poor, and he didn't want Ezra struggling for necessities when he grew up. Still, he could see his son's obsession as he continued to sketch and paint and Ezra's complete indifference to any other occupation.

Mr. Katz decided that if Ezra insisted on becoming an artist, he needed to see great art, so he took him on a father-son trip to the Metropolitan Museum of Art. Mr. Katz tilted his head and admired the majestic presidential presence as he pointed out the Gilbert Stuart portrait of George Washington. An unimpressed Ezra turned and looked down the white marble corridors and saw Honoré Daumier's *Third Class Carriage* framed in the archway. He found himself drawn down the hall toward the painting of poor, gaunt travelers in a simple wooden railway train and was transfixed as he observed light and dark play across perfectly ordinary people. He resolved to save money for carfare so he could return and gaze at the emerald green and earthy brown portrayal of weary, decent people sculptured from the light in the window.

At home, Ezra taught himself Daumier's style by copying his techniques and making reproductions of his paintings. When he was ready for an original, he knew some perfectly ordinary people to use for practice—his parents. They weren't proud of how they looked, and getting them to pose was difficult. His father said, "How about I get a shirt and tie. A jacket, maybe?"

Ezra said, "Those things aren't important. Remember at the Metropolitan Museum? A lot of paintings were of plain people."

Mr. Katz said, "I remember George Washington was dressed nice."

His mother had seen the reproductions of Daumier and Rembrandt. She ran her hands down her apron and looked down at its stains and her clumsy shoes, but she understood Ezra's need to paint real people in their own world. Finally, Ezra's parents agreed to pose, though his father remained suspicious as he stood shirtless in his long-john top with his suspenders hanging down behind. Using the lessons he had learned about light and dark from studying Daumier, Ezra painted his parents in the kitchen with the teakettle on the stove and a brown jug he'd found in the background. Sometimes they posed separately but when they had time, they posed together. Mr. Katz continued to fret. "What will people think?"

"Don't worry, Ben," said Mrs. Katz. "Just let him do what he has to do."

When the painting was finished, the three of them looked at it together. "Nice, very nice. Don't you think so, Ben?" asked Mrs. Katz.

"Hmmph. It's okay, I guess. But couldn't you make us a little more respectable?" Soon others would agree with his father.

Saturday was Ben's night off. As usual, friends and relatives gathered for piano playing and storytelling. Uncle Louie, sober for once, and Aunt Rosa in a black shawl joined the party. Mr. Katz was in a good mood and soon had everyone laughing at his story of Ezra's work as a sign painter, the trip to Greenwich Village, and the starving artists they saw.

"Don't forget the painting," said Mrs. Katz. "Ezra did a beautiful painting of us to show typical, plain people at home." And she hurried to get it.

A neighbor pointed out Mr. Katz's stomach in the painting. "Every man should have a little potbelly."

Uncle Louie said, "Don't you have a shirt? And what is that brown jug doing next to you?"

Aunt Rosa said, "Personally, I'm disappointed. If you ask me, when parents do what they can for a boy, even if it ain't much, the boy should make his parents look respectable and happy instead of like—"

"Failures," Uncle Louie finished.

Mr. Katz's face turned white. He opened his mouth to answer, but Mrs. Katz shook her head.

Ezra spoke up, "What's the disgrace in being poor? Wonderful people are poor." He lectured on and on about the paintings of Daumier and Rembrandt. He ended his tirade with, "Do you know why I'm painting those crappy signs? To get enough dough for paint and canvas. I'm going to be an artist and paint for those people, even if I do starve."

His father sat in silence, ghostly white. As people left, Ezra could hear Uncle Louie saying, "Failure," as they went down the stairs. The portrait, relegated to the closet, was mentioned afterward only when Aunt Rosa spread gossip about the ungrateful son in the neighborhood who had painted an awful picture of his loving parents. Mr. Katz seemed to give up on Ezra and sought solace in the company of old friends and the routines of work when he could get it.

Ezra sought acceptance outside his family. Jack, as he was known at Jefferson High School, found an appreciative audience in classmates, recognition in art venues for his talent, and encouragement from his young English teacher, Florence Freedman.

Mrs. Freedman first took note of Jack during a discussion of *Silas Marner*. Normally, the skinny, quiet boy sat in the last seat of the last row, but one day he startled her. Another student, following predictable thought, called Silas a miser because he hoarded his gold coins.

Jack rose to speak. "Silas Marner was not a miser. He loved beauty, and those gold coins were the only beauty he knew." He went on to explain that he saved his money and bought beautiful colors of paints one by one as he could afford them. He opened them, reveled in their beautiful colors, and screwed the tops back on. He counted them and put them away for safekeeping. He did not use them because he was not a good enough painter—yet. He finished, "If Silas Marner is a miser, I am, too." The students formed a bond with each other and with Mrs. Freedman.

After hearing about this favorite teacher for a while, Mrs. Katz decided she needed to meet her and sent an invitation for her to visit. Soon Mrs. Freedman stopped by on Friday afternoons for coffee, cake, or maybe orange Jell-O with whipped cream. She felt the warmth of the family as Mrs. Katz made a safe refuge for friends, neighbors, and relatives who joined them in the kitchen. This kitchen also served as a family room, with its Dutch look of sparkling white accented in Delft blue in its oilcloth table cover and dish towels. Perhaps the commonality of having immigrant parents overcame the distance in social and economic status between the two women. Only when Mr. Katz came home did Mrs. Freedman realize she'd stayed longer than she intended.

Mrs. Freedman found ways to encourage the promise she saw in Jack's paintings. Seeing how much he loved Daumier's work, she bought him his first book of art reproductions and a sketchbook. He kept the art book all his life and the sketchbook for twenty years until it fell apart. She made deals to trade his paintings for dental work from her husband—including a full set of false teeth for his mother, and she influenced one of her surgeon friends to take a painting in exchange for fixing Jack's nose from the fight with the bully.

In addition to the Depression in the United States, the world was in turmoil. Communism took hold in the USSR, Japan prepared to invade Manchuria, anti-Semitism increased in Germany, Poland, and Hungary. Soapbox lecturers on street corners invited heated arguments between speakers and audiences that sometimes led to violent exchanges.

People in the neighborhood heard news that Hitler had begun a purge of Jews. Stenciled leaflets urging people to come out and be counted were passed out on street corners and showed up on walls and lampposts. Children of immigrants like Mrs. Katz, who had known the terror of the pogroms, planned protest demonstrations. They learned songs and sang as they marched carrying banners.

"Down with Hitler."

"Stop Compromising."

"Save the Jews."

Jack found himself caught up in the excitement as he stepped off the curb and joined one of the marches. He didn't know what effect the demonstrations would have and wondered if Hitler would hear them. Still, his normally solitary self felt good in the midst of this great movement of people.

The National Student League planned an antiwar demonstration. The students would leave class at noon and go down to stand in silent protest against Mussolini's aggressions. Jack's father warned him to stay away from the peace demonstrations. He told Jack, "If I catch you with those Bolshevikies, I'll break every bone in your body. You stay in school, and mind your own business. I'm going to keep my eye on you. You hear?"

Noon approached on the day of the demonstration. It appeared to Jack that half the school was lined up in the halls and on the stairways waiting for the bell to ring. Out the window, he saw the policemen, some on horseback, who had heard about the planned demonstration. Jack was pinned against the door just before the bell rang. When the doors of the school opened, students behind him pushed him out in front. The crowd swarmed out behind him shouting, "Down with war and fascism!"

Jack's father stood across the street facing him. With his hands behind his back, Mr. Katz looked like the leader of all the policemen while Jack looked like the leader of the students. Seeing his father's stern face, he thought, "I'm in trouble." Then Mr. Katz grinned, shook his head from side to side, and walked away. Students sang protest songs, waved banners, and tossed leaflets into the air. When policemen swung their clubs to break up the crowd, the students threw their hands up to show that they were nonviolent. Slowly the policemen separated the demonstrators. They straggled off into small groups farther and farther from school.

Jack wandered home with one of his friends. Other friends joined them, and the friend's mother put cold compresses on their injuries. They spent the afternoon drinking lemonade and sharing their stories. Suddenly Jack was tired and knew he had to go home even though he was worried about what his family would say.

They were already eating supper when he walked in.

"You're late," his mother said. "Look at you. What happened? You were in that awful thing, weren't you?"

"Uh huh. I'm O.K."

His father broke in. "Stop. No arguments. We're eating." They ate supper in silence. When supper was over, Jack got up to leave the table. His eyes met his father's. His father gave him a weary smile. Jack needed to talk to Itch. He went out to find him. They spent the evening walking and talking—sharing their own secrets, hopes, and dreams—and their plan for saving the world. They dreamed of a time when there would be unemployment insurance, social security, health benefits, and some form of welfare for the hungry. They took hope when Franklin Delano Roosevelt became president. His father would later confide that he had voted for Eugene Victor Debs and later for Norman Thomas, leaders of the Socialist Party of America.

Some nights while they listened to the radio, Ezra watched his mother iron his father's shirts with flatirons. Even though Pete's Coffee Pot was just a rundown diner, Mr. Katz had to have a freshly laundered shirt every night for his work. Kelly would be out with his friends. Mae sat and sewed. His mother spit on the iron to see if it was hot enough and if not, it went back on the stove to heat some more. She moved back to the ironing board, listening as a rich voice sang, "Marta, rambling rose of the wildwood . . . all in vain I've been dreaming of a love light that's beaming . . ." Ezra watched her face turn young and pink. She stared into space and for a few minutes, she appeared to be somewhere else—somewhere with no worries about money, no floors to scrub, and no shirts to iron.

In the meanwhile, Jack continued to teach himself to paint using magazine covers from *Redbook*, *Cosmopolitan*, *Argosy*, and *The Literary Digest* for models. He painted scenes as far removed from his own life as the moon. There were lovely scenes of autumn leaves drifting down on quiet streets in New England with houses surrounded by trees and blue skies, unlike the tenements where he lived and pinched pennies. From *Argosy*, he painted a man in a seaman's hat at a pilot's wheel, making thousands of tiny dots with a pen.

In the world he knew, Jack believed that art could somehow relieve the cruelty of the Depression. His olfactory response to art as he examined American scenes painted by George Bellows brought a message of fragrance, a spirit released that he could smell and absorb in his body, giving him the idea that if people could see his art and sense the lives of those caught up in distress, perhaps they would develop pity and passion. His own passion, fed by being on relief and having to go for generic food, opened his eyes to common suffering and the indignities of the Depression.

Painting what he saw from his window, his tenements sandwiched themselves between a bit of gray sky and an empty lot. He went to the waterfront to paint the workers and to the government or charity handouts to portray people in breadlines. He saw people diseased, maimed, and unemployed and felt connected to them, people who did not belong as he felt he did not belong in his own family. His somber hues with just a bit of color in a small fire or a stove reflected the devastation of their lives. He hoped his paintings and those of others like him would produce empathy in the public and clear the world of its shadows. His painting was his own catharsis, giving him purpose and a place to take his own feelings of rejection.

By his final years of high school, Jack Katz was a recognized artist. He was elected president of the Brooklyn Young Artists and won a scholarship to the art branch of Educational Alliance. In April 1934, he won first place in the National Scholastic Competition sponsored by the Carnegie Foundation in an open competition for the United States and all its possessions for his painting *Shantytown*, featuring ordinary people and showing his compassion for those in the miseries of the Depression. The Carnegie Foundation sent the work on tour to leading art museums across the United States.

Reaching beyond his high school experience, Jack's work came to the attention of leading artists of the period. Max Weber, a pioneer of modernism in America under the influence of Pablo Picasso and George Braque, responded to a note from Keats with one of his own written in calligraphic-looking handwriting:

> 10 Hartley Road
> Great Neck, L. I.
> July 11, 1934

Dear Mr. Katz:

I received your kind note in due time, but left your note unanswered because of vague plans for a trip to Vermont—a trip I decided to take later in the summer.

Mrs. Weber and I will be pleased to have you come to see us. Next Saturday would be a nice day, and if you can arrange to come early in the day we would be pleased to have you stay for lunch.

There is a train at 11:05 leaving Pennsylvania Station—Long Island Division. You take train marked Port Washington—but you get off at Great Neck. Buy a return fair [sic] 65 cents, both ways. Train reaches Great Neck 11:43 and if you will write me that you are coming on that train I will be at the station to take you home. I wonder if you know me? On platform I will stand at entrance to taxi office near drug store. Will wear knickers.

Kindest regards

Max Weber

Astonished at receiving an invitation from such a renowned artist, Jack would learn later that some of his high school teachers had written Mr. Weber about him and sent samples of his work. Mr. Weber met him at the station on the appointed day and took him to a home that seemed exceptionally fine to this high school student who had grown up in the tenements. He treated Jack like a fellow painter, answering his questions about architectonics with examples and taking him to the site of his painting of the pond with the dead tree. They had lunch at a table with a linen tablecloth and napkins, appointed with elaborate table silver. The lunch conversation included stories of Weber's colleagues in Paris and his friendship with Rousseau. The heady experience concluded with a gift of a small painting of cherries signed, "a mon ami, Max Weber."

Articles about Jack's accomplishments ran in the *Red and White Publication* of his old school #149, in his high school paper *The Liberty Bell*, in the *New York Times*, and in the Jewish newspapers. They lauded his mural called *Labor* on the second floor of the Thomas Jefferson building, his one-man show hosted by the Carnegie Foundation, and his upcoming art scholarships, and they noted his contact with leading artists Max Weber and Abbo Ostrowsky.

Neighbors and relatives greeted Jack's father with congratulations when they read the news items. Mr. Katz just shrugged. Even his mother didn't talk much about his art anymore. At home, Jack painted quietly and stashed his work away.

As Jefferson High School's graduation neared in January 1935, Jack was alerted that he would receive the medal for the best artist in his graduating class, necessitating an appearance on stage to receive the award. For days, he worried about the public appearance, wishing something would happen, that maybe somebody would get sick and he wouldn't have to show up.

At noon on the day before graduation, Jack and his mother were in the kitchen. Thinking about lunch, his mother asked,

"How about an omelet?" Before he could answer, there was a knock at the door.

Mrs. Katz opened the door, and a man asked, "Is your son the artist at home? We have some burlap for his painting."

Ezra was surprised to see one of his father's buddies from the shoemaker's store, a man who often sat around in a group telling stories from the old countries. The shoemaker never saved burlap for him. "You gotta get it right away," the man said, "or they'll throw it out."

Mrs. Katz went back to making lunch. The man whispered, "I gotta talk to you."

When Ezra came outside on the landing, the man said, "Your father—he's very sick. He's across the street by Harry the shoemaker."

"Is he dead?"

The man trembled. "Yes." But Ezra already knew.

His mother called, "Your lunch'll get cold."

Ezra said, "He's in a hurry. I've got to get the burlap right away."

"Put something on. It's freezing out there."

Ezra grabbed his coat and hurried downstairs and out into a bad snowstorm. When he walked into the shoemaker's shop, Ezra saw his father stretched out in a little booth, his tattered gray coat that he often lined with newspapers to keep warm thrown over him, and the worn soles of his shoes sticking out.

A policeman asked, "Will you identify the body?"

Ezra could have distinguished him from shoe soles alone, the same ones that caused the arguments at home. "He's my father."

The policeman searched Mr. Katz's pockets, found his billfold, and handed it to Ezra. "Check the wallet."

Ezra opened it and took out two one-dollar bills and multiple worn folded newspaper clippings from the *Daily News*, the *New York Times*, and the *Jewish Daily Forward*—tattered notices of awards he'd won, one with his photo. Ezra realized they had been unfolded and refolded many times as his father took them out to show his friends.

In the trip with his father to the art museum, he had made a significant discovery of the artist Daumier. Now he was making another discovery. His father had shared the story of the angel making the cleft in his chin. His father had repeated often, "You'll starve. You'll live like a bum. Don't I work in Greenwich Village?" His father brought home paints and brushes for him to use. Now, here were these treasured clippings. Ezra put all the pieces together and realized not only was his father terrified that he would lead a life of hardship, but his father had been exceedingly proud of him.

Ezra went back to break the news to his mother, starting the conversation several times, hinting that his father was not well. He hoped she would ask, but she did not. Finally, Ezra said, "He is dead."

His mother asked, "How will we tell Mae?"

The massive snowstorm ended the day of the funeral. Three old cars made a funeral procession that slid and skidded over the frozen ground to the cemetery. Gravediggers had dug the grave through the deep snow and frozen dirt. They lowered the casket into the ground among the snow-covered tombstones, and mourners threw pieces of earth on top of the coffin before the gravediggers shoveled snow and dirt on top of the grave.

Ezra wandered off, leaned against a tree, and cried. Someone called, "Come back to the car."

He looked up at a branch where snow mounded atop each leaf. Suddenly one of the leaves bent down, dropping its load of snow to the ground. The leaf moved back up into its place—relieved of its burden, but bare. Ezra did not miss the symbolism. He would move on without the burden of his father's fear, but empty of his father's secret pride.

CHAPTER 6

*U*NCERTAIN *D*AYS

THE KATZ FAMILY DELAYED THEIR WORRIES DURING THE TIME they sat Shiva, the week set aside after the funeral for mourning and prayers for Benjamin. They draped white sheets across their mirrors according to their tradition, so no one could look at himself or herself in vanity, and sat in slippered feet on boxes, crates, and short stools low to the ground to show the discomfort of sorrow and waited for visitors to come and bring comfort. Few people ventured out on the icy roads, but Uncle Louie and Aunt Rosa lived close and trudged up the windy snow-covered street.

The upstairs neighbor, Mrs. Love, rushed in, dressed all in black. "Poor Ben! Poor Gussie!" she exclaimed. She rushed over to Ezra, who sat on a stool, hugged and kissed him, and wailed. "Ezra, you're an orphan. Try not to cry. You're a man now."

Ezra bolted to the bathroom for refuge and locked the door, but as he turned, he found Uncle Louie already there. They wept together. Uncle Louie cried for Benjamin and for the guilt he shared with Ezra for not liking Benjamin while he was living. He cried for Ezra and for himself, the family drunk. Finally, he whispered, "One thing that ya Pa was right about. Don't be an artist—another bum in the family." Aunt Rosa came to the bathroom looking for Uncle Louie and led him out.

When Shiva ended, the financial situation had to be faced. Mrs. Katz had never held a paying job. Her family work had been scrubbing floors and washing clothes with a rubboard. Mae's back problem gave her few options, and her small salary as a bookkeeper would hardly pay the bills.

Kelly planned to get married—another distress. Not only would he not be making much contribution to the family budget, but his family members were nervous about how a wedding celebration would look. Eastern European Jewish tradition called for a year of mourning after a parent died, and words would be said, "The ground hasn't cooled yet, and he is getting married." In addition to embarrassing the family with a wedding, supporting a wife would leave little extra from his salary, despite Kelly's promises to help. Ezra felt the responsibility falling on his shoulders and knew he would need to make a living instead of using the two art school scholarships he had received.

He searched the classifieds in the newspaper as Jack, joining what he called "the vast army of the unemployed." He answered an ad from a comic book artist wanting a cleanup and background man. When he called for an appointment, the artist, not wanting to ruin his prized brushes, told Jack to bring his own. Jack traveled all the way into Manhattan, where the artist took him down into a studio, dimly lit with one light bulb. For almost an hour, Jack squinted and inked in drawings. He used a process known as feathering, starting with a thin line and then thicker and thicker, another thin line and then thicker and thicker until it formed a turn where the darker areas met and became a form.

As he worked, he thought about the great artists he had imitated—El Greco, Van Gogh, Modigliani. For some reason, these comics that he saw as corny and cliched gave him more trouble than those great artists. He had worked up a sweat, his eyes hurt, and his hand cramped.

After almost an hour, the man came back. He looked at Jack's work. "No, it won't do."

Feeling defeated, Jack cleaned his brushes, stood up, and put on his jacket. The man said, "I'm sorry, I can't use you. You owe me fifteen cents."

Jack asked, "For what?"

"The ink."

Jack left his first job interview fifteen cents poorer than he had started.

In the meantime, Jack joined other embarrassed recipients of relief checks in a slowly recovering depression economy that once reached about 25 percent unemployment. His card information read, "Jack Katz, 19, 5' 11", brown hair, grey eyes, white." The reverse side of the card warned in three languages "Do not surrender this card to anyone except the proper relief officer. This card must be shown in order to receive your check. This card must be used as identification to cash your check." His address was listed as 214 Blecker Street, Brooklyn, New York.

In June 1935, he received a letter granting him a scholarship in the New York High School competition for free tuition to any one of the winter classes from September 16, 1935 to May 29, 1936 with a list of instructors. Underlined in the list was, "Kenneth Hayes Miller," an artist who taught at the Art Students League for forty years encouraging students to find their art in the Renaissance and in contemporary urban life.

Jack's reputation earned him an invitation to put up an exhibit at the Art Teacher's Conference and another to a WPA (Works

Progress Administration) "New Horizons' Greatest Art Show of 1936." A promotional statement included in their brochure said, "A number of new names made their appearance in the local art world during the year, names we will hear more of each season from now on."

Jack found other odd jobs doing background for comics until some of his old friends from his high school art club told him about a new venture called Five Star Comics. Harry Chesler, the owner, supplied comic book content to publishers as a packager in the new medium. His friends helped Jack prepare samples, coached him to know what to ask for as a salary, and introduced him to the boss.

Harry watched him draw. "That's very nice, son," he said. Instead of offering Jack a salary, he asked, "How much do you want a week?"

Jack looked over at the other guys, bent over the tables drawing comics. "Twenty dollars," he said.

Harry said, "That's a lotta money. The best I can offer is eighteen dollars, fifty cents."

Jack pretended to consider. "Okay, $18.50."

Harry said, "Settled. You can start Monday."

Jack began work on Monday in the loft filled with rows of drawing tables with seating on wooden boxes. Men and women worked on pages twice the size of comic books. Only the cleanup man who erased pencil lines and whited out errors had a lower job. Jack inked in background items, the buildings, trees, cars, and other vehicles, while hoping for upward mobility to the stage of drawing actual characters, and ultimately as a master artist to collaborate with the writers for figures, lighting, and background—the whole scene.

Jack received his first paycheck on Friday and counted it carefully.

"Boss," he said, "there's a mistake here. I got nineteen bucks."

Harry said, "That ain't no mistake, Son. I been watchin' you. You're doin' okay. That's a raise. First week you're working here, and you got a raise already."

The next Friday, Jack counted his money and there was $19.50. He said, "Boss, it's $19.50."

Harry said, "Right. Another raise. See? You worked here two weeks and you got two raises already. You didn't even have to ask for it. Right?"

The third week, Jack had twenty dollars, so he pointed that out to the boss.

Harry said, "That's right. Three weeks and three raises. No other studio is as generous as I am. Have you ever heard of such a thing?"

Jack admitted he never had.

Harry raised his voice so all the workers could hear, "I want you to understand something. I gave you a raise because right now, I can afford it. But, please, don't ever ask me for a raise. If I can give it to you, I'll give it to you. If I can't, I won't. So, do me a favor. Don't ever ask for more raises. You'll only hurt my feelings."

Harry smoked stinky cigars and spit a lot, spraying the air with tobacco bits. When he stood behind Jack, a gray shape appeared on the drawing board above a clean outline of Jack's head and shoulders. It was not hard for Jack to figure out where the rest of the spittle went when he felt it behind his right ear. He wondered if he smelled like stale tobacco smoke when they finished the conversation, but Harry stopped spraying him when Jack brought the problem to his attention.

A compassionate boss, Harry allowed one of his workers to bring in his baby when his wife left him and the infant behind. Harry even played with the child and discussed the difficulties of bringing up kids with the father. When his workers began adding an extra five minutes and then ten to their half-hour lunch break, Harry became creative and made a suggestion that was really a command, asking his workers to consider bringing in their sandwiches every day. He would furnish coffee and pickles. Harry filled coffee cups like a benign waiter every day until the exact moment of the half-hour lunch was up and work began again.

Jack inked over the pencil lines and shaded the pictures. He drew backgrounds with mountains and airwaves where good guys single-handedly triumphed over evil, stopped all the wars, and brought peace. With a kindly boss and congenial coworkers, life became a bit easier, but he knew drawing Chesler's creepy comics was not art. Once again, doubts about his talent crept into Jack's mind. Maybe he was not even an artist.

At home, Ezra faced his canvas and examined his paintings. His hands began to shake, he got nauseous, and he felt a chill from the rejection of his own work. He looked at all his paintings and saw ugliness. "Who am I fooling?" he thought to himself. "These are terrible." He slashed them with a knife. Rip! Rip! Rip! As he grew angrier and angrier, his slashes got bigger and bigger. He kicked his foot through them, cracking the wooden stretchers until he heard a whimper behind him.

"Stop!" cried Mae, "Stop. Please, stop."

Mae sat and cried, showing feelings Ezra had never seen. He didn't know she cared about his paintings. Exhausted, he dropped his knife and went out the door, leaving the debris behind. When he came back, the mess had been cleaned up. It would be several years before he began to paint seriously again.

Mae died many years later in her home a few blocks from Kelly in Florida. Kelly went through her apartment, sorting what to keep and what to throw away. He found the paintings and asked Ezra about them. Mended with tape and Mae's stitching, Ezra saw his familiar paintings patched and preserved to the best of his sister's ability with surgery performed by the same needles that had tormented him as a child.

During this time when Ezra had stopped painting, he worked at unfulfilling jobs and avoided friends. In addition to his own hopelessness, his mother's health was failing. Mrs. Katz had to rest more often. Ezra knew his mother, who had worked hard all her life, wouldn't be content sitting doing nothing. He brought her some canvas and paints and recommended that she try to paint something.

She protested in the beginning, but then Ezra suggested that she paint something to go in the nursery for the baby Mrs. Freedman was expecting soon. He came home one day and found she'd painted two children on a park bench with beautiful lifelike grass. He questioned how she'd learned to do that. She answered, "I didn't know how to paint grass, so I looked through your art books. That Van Gogh—he does the best grass, so I copied him." Ezra was not the only member of his family to teach himself to paint well. Mrs. Freedman liked this painting and others that Mrs. Katz did for her son's nursery so much that she saved them to the next generation for her grandson. Itch's mother was more impressed with Mrs. Katz's paintings than with Ezra's since she had had no opportunity to study art.

Over the next few years, Jack's goal of becoming an artist dimmed. He drifted from job to job almost as often as he changed apartments, and he lived at eight addresses between March 1935 and June 1939. Nighttime found him at Ardie's small luncheonette at tables with friends, smoking cigarettes bought singly from packages with a match for one cent, in discussions about neighborhood gossip, work, and politics.

Eventually that group broke up, and he signed up for a life painting class in the neighborhood at Greenwich House. He'd never drawn from a live model before and became unnerved when the model dropped her robe. He learned some new things but became frustrated by the art teacher's rules and regulations, with the lack of joy the teacher exhibited, and the large class. He and one of his classmates, Jackson Pollock, who would become a creative leader in the abstract Expressionist movement, left the class.

Jack tried going to therapists. Some were helpful, and then there were the others. One therapist's walls were lined with diplomas and certificates in English and German and with works by famous artists. If he began to talk about women, she assured him she did not want to hear about his love life. She advised him to read British newspapers because they were objective and businesslike and would regulate his temperament. He did follow that suggestion by subscribing to a couple of British newspapers. He found them fascinating and felt they did calm him down.

At the end of one counseling session, he walked around to get a closer look at her artwork and discovered the names of Degas, Goya, Rubens, Modigliani, and Whistler, each signature painted by the same hand with the same thickness of a burnt umber brush. He called her attention to the resemblance and added that the Whistler in the foyer did not have his signature butterfly with the stinging tail. She explained that the painting came from an early period before the artist began using the symbol.

Jack questioned the painting signed by Rubens that was unlike any of his other work. She said it was done when he was very young before he developed his style. Not willing to leave the

subject alone, Jack offered to ask a friend of his who worked at
the Metropolitan Museum to authenticate the paintings. She
refused, citing that she had bought all of them from someone
who dealt exclusively in examples of early work of famous artists.

Jack found her therapy equally unreliable. She didn't believe
in Freudian analysis and wanted to spend no time talking about
his sex life. She recommended that he pursue an active social life,
and to that end, she suggested that they go to a movie together.
He didn't remember the movie they saw but did remember her
thanking him for a lovely evening.

The last straw came at his next appointment. In answer to her
inquiry, Jack admitted that he had begun to draw again. She hurried to get a book that she had found useful and thought would
be helpful to him. He waited to open the book on his way home.
Leafing through, he found shapes to use in drawing animals.
With two small circles for eyes inside a larger circle for the face
with two triangles on top for ears and with the addition of a few
whiskers, the artist had a cat. In one last session, he returned the
book and never went back, assuming her professional expertise
equaled her artistic knowledge. Years later, he received a letter
with her compliments on one of his book jackets and her affir-
mation that his drawing was fine now.

Jack took his sketching to the cafeterias and the subways—
to a city waiting to be drawn—working people, artists, tourists,
addicts, derelicts. On the weekend, he went back to the waterfront
and breadlines and discovered that hunger had no color lines.
Many of the unemployed were well educated, some with lost
legs from hopping freights, and others living under the docks.
He sketched in Grand Central and Penn stations and watched
the people.

Identifying with the hoboes and the unemployed, he saw an
unshaven man with his hat over his face looking for a handout

at a Greek restaurant. The owner offered a roll and some soup. Jack handed him a menu and said, "Why don't you have dinner. It's on me." The vision of the man with his head in his hands, sobbing in relief, etched itself into Jack's memory.

In the meantime, Itch attended tuition-free City College. For the first three years, he had little time to spend with Ezra. His study load lightened the last year, and once again he had time for his friend. Sometimes they visited an art museum, with Ezra sharing his love of art. He made Itch stand with his nose so close to a painting that he could see the brush strokes and how one color was laid across another to make the picture.

When they took walks by the sea, Ezra would tell Itch to look at the colors. Itch looked and saw blue. "Keep looking," Ezra would say. "You'll see red if you look long enough." Itch looked again and saw blue. He looked and looked, and then he saw it. In the little grooves as the waves crested, there was red. Just like boyhood times, they talked and walked each other home.

Not quite ready to give up his dream, Ezra began again to practice in his own paintings what he and Itch had seen. He clipped interesting images from magazines that gave him painting ideas and models for his pictures, including one from *Life* magazine for 13 May 1940, with a series of pictures of a little Black boy in Liberty County, Georgia. The description of the sequence by the editor who submitted it from the *Quitman Free Press* in Georgia said the boy was participating in a blood test of schoolchildren for a malaria survey. The captions on the pictures read:

"The boy is carefree at first."

"He asks if the test will hurt."

"Trustingly he holds out his hand."

"Test hurt and he starts to cry."

Jack liked that little boy. He clipped the pictures and put them on his bulletin board. For the next twenty years, the clipping would rotate between the bulletin board and a drawer where he kept special items that he liked, little knowing just how important these photos would become.

Gradually, Jack moved up to what he saw as the ultimate job in the comics world. He was hired by Fawcett Publications to work on Captain Marvel. Once again, he had to start at the bottom. He did background. Then he was promoted to drawing secondary people. Finally, he was allowed to ink in Captain Marvel, but not yet his head. With a sheet of statistics showing Captain Marvel's head in every direction, Jack studied the distance between the eyebrows, the placement of the nose, the shape of the chin. He studied width and height for the position of the facial features so he would be ready when he was allowed to draw Captain Marvel, and he practiced.

At night, after work, he often walked along the streets with Itch, adding political concerns in Europe and Asia to their personal conversations. Attacks on Jews increased as Hitler took over Germany and Stalin instituted purges in the Soviet Union. The Japanese seized cities in China, and Franco was winning the war against the legal democratic republic in Spain.

Interrupting these serious talks, neighborhood children pointed to Jack and whispered to each other, "He draws Captain Marvel." From time to time, he brought home copies of the issues he'd worked on and showed them which pictures he drew or brought them discarded pages. Jack enjoyed being the neighborhood hero and hoped soon to bring them a sample of his drawing of the captain's face.

On 7 December 1941, just when Fawcett Publications was ready for him to draw Captain Marvel, Jack and Itch were walking together in Greenwich Village and heard the news that Japan had attacked Pearl Harbor. The friends separated as they joined the war effort, with Itch going to the Far East and Ezra to Tampa, Florida.

Jack, as he would be known in the military, entered the Third Air Force Division of the Army on 13 April 1943. The Army used his artistic talents as a draftsman working on camouflage. He drew charts for statistical control, painted pictures for posters, and made booklets for camouflage training. He qualified for a rifle marksmanship badge and advanced from private to corporal.

In the different world he found in Tampa, his fellow soldiers came from many places and many walks of life with totally different interests and opinions. To mitigate their loneliness, the men became temporary family, staying up late talking. Jack could relate to a few who shared his dreams for the brotherhood of man or who made good drinking buddies. At this point, the number of stripes on their sleeves marked the only difference among them, although in later years when they attempted a reunion in their assorted clothes and with their various backgrounds, they found themselves with nothing to talk about.

Merchants routinely charged the GIs more than local residents for any purchases they made. They might sell a belt to a local customer for $2 but charge a soldier $3.50. On Sundays after a payday, the soldiers might go out to eat in a restaurant in their required freshly laundered uniforms and a tie, but they soon saw that no Blacks were allowed in the restaurants. Since the Army was not yet integrated, he and all his white cronies were allowed to eat.

For a relaxing Sunday afternoon, Jack asked permission to borrow a jeep and gathered a group of soldiers who were interested in learning to paint. He drove until he found a vista conducive to painting lessons. Art-worthy scenery was easy to find along the Hillsborough River or Tampa Bay.

One Sunday he had an intruder. The painters hopped off the truck, but this big guy continued to sit, saying, "I just came for the ride." Jack was furious. He was not having anybody who came along just for the ride. The guy had brought no materials for painting, so Jack handed him a pad of paper and a pencil, insisting that he sketch. The man returned from Sunday to Sunday, took up painting as well as sketching, and came to appreciate Jack for showing him the power to put what he saw into a picture.

A good day might bring a letter from Itch written during a ten-minute break in one of his military courses. He told of the tension as fellows were notified to appear before the board with warnings that 20 percent of them would wash out (i.e., fail) and reassured Ezra that he had not been called to appear. He noted that the great majority of the officers had come from the ranks, refuting the idea that common people lacked talent for leadership. He filled the rest of the letter with friendly chitchat about daily routines, a planned trip home, and meeting acquaintances they both knew.

Jack was still in Tampa in 1945 when World War II ended with the surrender of Germany in May and Japan in July. In October, Mae sent a lengthy appeal for Corporal Jack Katz's release from the armed forces, explaining her struggle to pay the bills and care for her mother, who was suffering from "a very bad gall bladder condition, heart trouble, and high blood pressure." The drugs given for her gall bladder attacks required someone to lift her and help her move. Mae noted that her own curvature of the spine made her handicapped for such work and added that the doctor had prescribed better care and more personal attention than she was able to give since her employment left her mother alone all day. She reasoned that Jack's additional salary if he could return home would enable them to get better care for their mother and help pay off debts incurred with the medical bills. She added that the Red Cross helped pay the bills for seven months and scribbled a note in the margin that her average salary was twenty-nine dollars a week.

Their rabbi sent a letter confirming that the burden of support for Mrs. Katz had fallen on Mae, who had a limited income, and noted that their situation had become so dire that they were affected both mentally and physically. He added that Corporal Katz "desires in no way to shirk his responsible duties to his country for his 2 & ½ yr. in service will prove that he has been loyal, devoted, & conscientious." He reiterated Mae's claim that Mrs. Gussie Katz has suffered with gall bladder attacks and a bad heart with the burden of support falling on Mae since Jack had been in the Army, and added the necessity of their having to borrow money to ease them over their economic difficulties.

The letters accomplished their purpose, and Jack received his discharge from the Army on 24 November 1945, earning a Good Conduct Medal, an American Theater Ribbon, and the Victory Medal.

LOOKING FOR HIMSELF

IN THE DIFFERENT WORLD TO WHICH HE RETURNED, JACK found himself alone and unemployed. His old friends had moved, married, or just not returned from the Army. He rented a room for five dollars a week in a little family house on Perry Street in the Village. Included in his rent was maid service and a change of sheets; not included was heat in the bedroom. If he wanted heat, he had to leave the bedroom door open to the bathroom, which also served as the entrance into his room. Still, he found the small room a pleasant upgrade from being in the barracks living with thirty or forty guys.

The family had a four-year-old son named Steven who came into his room in the mornings and whispered into Jack's mouth, "Are you awake yet?" Then he'd say, "Tell me a story." In a bit of foreshadowing of what the future held for him, Jack told him stories, and they became buddies.

Jack's childhood health problems continued, and he spent the month of June 1946 in the Veteran's Administration Hospital. The VA declared him 20 percent disabled from a duodenal ulcer and 10 percent from an unspecified "nervous condition."

Soon Itch returned home as well, and the men picked up their friendship where they'd left off. Both of them were interested in what was happening in the world and often attended lectures followed by lively discussions. One night, Itch brought along Lillie Bellin, his girlfriend, having told her he wanted her to meet a special friend. Happily, Lillie and Ezra became close friends as well. When Itch and Lillie married later that year with a reception spread of delicious food, Ezra's ulcer compelled him to watch everybody eat while he stuck with milk and crackers.

Working in his little room and hoping to get contracts, Jack painted samples for advertisers and received an assignment for a full-color editorial in *Collier's* magazine. A menswear editor gave him another assignment for a spread on the newest fad— Bermuda shorts. Jack researched and found a picture of a famous church with twin towers rising behind a hill in Bermuda. On pastel paper with tempera paint, he put his duplicating skills to work and drew the road heading over the hill. He conjured up a handsome guy in an open-necked short-sleeved shirt and Bermuda shorts and painted him strolling down the road beside a flagstone fence.

When he brought in his finished work, the editor examined it closely, "Oh, that's very good. You did a nice job. I know that church. I've been to Bermuda." Then he paused, "You know, that church should be just a little closer to the road. Move it over to the left a little."

Jack took the painting home and faced an impossible task. The editor wanted it back on Monday, but he couldn't erase on the pastel paper that formed the background color. To make the change would require doing the whole painting over, and there was not enough time. Jack waited until Monday and took the painting back to the editor.

The editor inspected it. "That's much better. Much better," he said.

Jack struck up a friendship with a rather striking young woman named Rosalie who lived in the next-door room. By the time she moved out and got a small apartment, their relationship had developed to the point that Jack moved in with her and shared the expenses using his nighttime freelancing money. He enjoyed the domesticated setting of shopping for groceries and preparing meals, visiting her friends, and having them over for dinner. When he brought her home to meet his family, his mother's questioning divulged that she was not Jewish, that she had been divorced, and that they were living together. Gussie let him know that she did not approve.

Hoping to eliminate one of his difficulties with the signs he frequently encountered saying, "No Jews hired here," Jack petitioned to change his name from Jacob Ezra Katz to the less Jewish-sounding name of Ezra Jack Keats. While some would ascribe his choice of names to the Endymion quote from John Keats's poem that graced his high school auditorium, most likely, he followed in his brother Kelly's footsteps who had already taken Keats for a last name. He morphed into the new last name, but for the rest of his life, depending on how people knew him, his first name would waffle between "Ezra" and "Jack."

Gussie Katz died 8 May 1948. Mae, who was alone with their mother, heard her call out, "Help me!"

Terrified, Mae called for the doctor and wrung her hands crying, "What can I do?" Gussie tried to sit up and gasped, "Do something!" Mae kissed her, and for the first time she could remember, her mother did not turn away from the kiss. Gussie died of a heart attack before the doctor could get there.

Along with his money problems, Jack's relationship with Rosalie became rocky, and now with the ambivalent grief that he must have felt after his mother's death, he became depressed. Jack wondered if Kelly could help him.

By this time, Jack had figured out that Kelly hadn't abandon him or the family when he married and had come to understand that Kelly had a right to his own happiness. His sister-in-law Millie was kind to Jack, often talking to him about his family. She helped him see that his parents' and siblings' lives had also been difficult and helped him understand that they had really loved him. Kelly owned a successful photofinishing shop where he developed and processed film, and Mae worked for him in his specialty of tinting photographs with fine cotton swabs.

Jack told Kelly, "I've got to get out of this country; I just want to leave and get away from everything." Kelly worried about him and loaned Jack two thousand dollars to go to Europe and study art in Paris. Years later when Jack was able to repay him, Kelly had forgotten about the loan.

Jack contacted the Académie de la Grande Chaumière and received a reply in October 1948 that he would be accepted under the bill of rights, assuring him that his qualifications were quite sufficient. They included information on lodging and said that painting, sculpture, and drawing courses were offered year round. He brushed up on his high school French and sent for a passport.

In his trip diary beginning 13 April 1949, Jack described his departure. A small group of friends, including Itch and Rosalie, came to wish him bon voyage before he sailed out on the SS *Washington*. He found it tortuous to kiss Rosalie good-bye and bid farewell to warm friends. Itch and Rosalie bent over the railings, waving and throwing kisses until he was out of sight. Jack cried as he paced the deserted top deck in the fog and rain, unexpectedly dwelling on the good times, regretting that he was leaving Rosalie behind, and wondering if he should have insisted that she not come to see him off.

The next day's diary entry reflected a better mood, as he began an account of the people he met on the ship. A Frenchman had lived in New York for a year and was anxious to return for another visit. Having experienced the privations of postwar France, the man filled his plate with as much food as he could eat at mealtimes.

Jack bonded with the steward on the boat, who shared his interest in art and was a big admirer of artists Ludwig Bemelmans and Andrew Loomis, a pair that Jack found to be a strange combination. The steward showed his own artwork to Jack and shared his dream of quitting the sea and using his savings to study art in France. He philosophized that making money was useless if you had to turn around and spend the money to do what you really liked. Jack recorded the conversation in his diary, maybe because it supported his own longing to become an artist. The next day Jack shared his own paintings with the steward, who responded with much admiration before asking if he was too old at thirty-nine to develop his art and make a living at it. Jack did not record his answer, perhaps because he questioned his own single-minded effort to make a living with art that still had him struggling at thirty-three.

Other companions on the ship were quite varied and included Irish, Scottish, and French nationalities, with ages ranging from young children to old men. A Scotsman entertained with bagpipes on the deck, marching with pride and dignity in a dancelike step. The rage among the French was "Buttons and Bows" and what Jack classified as "other hillbilly songs."

By the third day, Jack was ready for the trip on the stinky ship to be over. Odors of the next meal permeated the air at all times, and his mind kept returning to Rosalie and wondering how they had loused things up.

On 19 April, he spotted Ireland and recorded that the surrounding water as well as the island was green. The ship that came to offload the passengers who had reached their destination brought hawkers selling rosaries, newspapers, scarves, and other mementos. The newspapers they brought aboard carried stories of strong demonstrations and fights with police. In the distance, he saw yellow-brown houses and a tall cathedral.

The ship docked in France on 20 April. Jack described what he saw in the first of several letters to Rosalie: "Wednesday morning, we docked at Le Havre. It looked so wounded and sad. The bombings wrecked this port. Everyone on deck looked on in impressive silence although when they sighted the place from the distance, they had been quite noisy and gay."

Jack rode the train from Normandy, watching the panorama out his window until they reached new scenes in Paris. A gendarme directed traffic with his white stick as cars raced in all directions. Jack heard a strange honking of horns and the tinkling of many bicycle bells and wondered for a moment where he had heard all these sounds before until he realized the scenes had been in Gershwin's *American in Paris*. All the French movies and printings he had seen suddenly became three dimensional.

He took a taxi to his room at the Pension Jeanne. The cab driver coughed around his cigarette and asked if this was Jack's first visit to Paris. Jack answered that it was his very first. The cab driver talked the rest of the way, but Jack didn't understand a word. Instead of trying to carry on a conversation, he took a memory trip back to his discovery of the art books in a Brooklyn library and felt that Lautrec, Utrillo, Degas, and many others were beckoning him. The French Impressionists had called to him since he had found their art as a boy in the Arlington Branch of the public library. Now here he was, looking out through his taxi window on the city bathed in the blue-gray dusk that had just been liberated from the Nazis.

The driver deposited Jack and his Army footlocker, packed with all his worldly goods, in front of the pension where he would stay. The porter helped him carry the footlocker up to a room papered in pink and white flowers. The tiny room had a table, a chair, a single bed, a closet with tall mirrors, and a sink. The bathroom was down the hall. But his view from the French windows was superb, looking out on a court and beyond to orange and terra cotta rooftops with chimneys and chimney pots.

Dashing out into Boulevard du Montparnasse, Jack pulled the beret he had bought on the ship off his head and threw it in the air. He smelled tobacco and coffee and heard sounds of honking horns and clattering plates mingled with talking and laughter. He walked past poster-plastered walls, kiosks, and flower stalls. He saw someone's shadow stretching ahead of him on the cobblestone streets and was surprised to find it was his own. After reading about it all his life, he was on the streets of Montparnasse—in Paris at last. He finally wended his way back through the people who still filled the streets to the pension. It was 2:45 AM.

After the chambermaid brought his breakfast of rolls and coffee, he wolfed down his food and headed back out to observe the street cleaner, dressed in a blue smock and wooden shoes, as he watered down and swept the streets. He listened in on two unkempt women standing in their bathrobes and was surprised to hear them speaking Yiddish.

Supper and breakfast were included in his rent, so he made sure to be present at meals. Conversation at the supper table revealed that only about ten words of his French were understandable. In postwar Paris, only luxury hotels had fine food. His lacked flavor, so he gathered his courage and asked the waitress for some "sal."

"Eh?" she said.

Jack repeated. "Sal. Sal." Smiles spread across the faces around the table.

Finally, one of the young men snapped, "You know what he means. Why don't you get it?"

She brought the "sel"—salt, even though Jack had asked for "sal"—dirty.

The young man, Roger, became an instantaneous friend, but it would be a while before he told Jack his story in hushed tones. Roger's parents were Jewish and had been hidden by the Jeanne family at the risk of their own lives during the Nazi occupation. Since Roger never talked about them in the present, Jack assumed they had been rounded up and killed. Perhaps Jack's memory of his own mother's story of escaping the pogroms led him to that conclusion and made him reticent to intrude to ask for the rest of Roger's history.

Without delay, Jack visited the Louvre, entering the immense grounds with a feeling that he knew the building and maybe had been there before. He recounted that visit and his impressions of his first day of observing Parisian life in his diary. He tingled with amazement as he walked through what he deemed the Great Mecca of Art and in wonder that his difficult times had brought him to this place. Evaluating artists as he went, he saw a lack of definition in the form of Da Vinci, a kind of pudginess, and thought it less than the color and drama of Titian. He found the original Veronese *Crucifixion* to be a revelation and was amazed at its difference from the reproduction he owned. The *Mona Lisa* seemed to capture a moment of mystery in the unanswered question that was Leonardo himself. But the high point for him was El Greco's painting *Christ on the Cross Adored by Two Donors*. He felt himself on a cloud and subject to swooning.

Outside on the streets, he watched the parade for the Partisans for Peace. Resistance fighters, old workers, miners, Italians, Greeks, Dutch, and others piled in garbage trucks to demonstrate.

On the corner, a flower vendor and a newspaper vendor sat at a table and a French couple sipped wine in front of a traffic cop among rows of trees and houses. The flower vendor sat with his back to his business, popping up when his friends called his attention to a customer to run over and make his sale before returning to his conversation and the newspaper he'd borrowed from a friend. When he finished, he returned the paper to the newspaperman, who straightened it out and put it back on his stand. Shortly, the news vendor became distracted by a wedding procession coming out from across the street, with the bride in her veil and girls in blue and white.

Soon Jack settled into a routine. He wore a French beret while he sketched and painted during the day. Five nights a week, he studied French. He spent hours in the multitude of French museums gazing at paintings and sculpture. He walked the city streets and found time to go and place a rose on Modigliani's grave. War-torn Paris seemed to be an echo of the grand city he'd always heard about, but he noticed that art exhibits received more attention than commercial advertising. He did seven paintings during his first two and a half weeks in Paris, but none of them came out to his satisfaction. Still, he found life less stressful than in New York.

In Jack's second letter to Rosalie, dated 10 May, he gives an update on his adjustment. He mentions that she is the one and only person with whom he can be perfectly honest about the good and bad parts of being alone in a new place. He added that, despite initial misgivings, he was now sure he'd made the right decision to come.

He had moved to a fifth-floor room, larger and with more light but still not a studio. He had hopes of getting one in August, when the people who lived there went to Italy; this had two conditions, first if he could increase his income and second if the family remained in Italy, which they had planned to do. He recounted roughing it with little eating out and minimal entertainment because of expenses.

He told her his time was taken up with painting most of the day, studying French, and observing at the plentiful museums. Paris did not compare to New York, nor was it the vision he had expected from his studies of the French artists. He described it as an echo of the grand glittering city that got caught up in the throes of war. Closing this section of the letter, he said, "Paris in the moment looks like a slightly worn and tired woman—yet singing."

Ending the letter, apparently with an answer to her suggestion that she might join him, he estimated that she could get along with $130 a month if she was willing to live as he did and assured her that he would not be allowed to share his single room with her unless the studio came through later. He reported that jobs were scarce and hard to get, with much adjustment to the difference in culture. After this bit of discouragement to any plan she had to come to France, he closed with lighthearted questions about New York, her job, and her friends.

Before his formal classes began, Jack made a quick trip to London and wandered around for several days surveying the damage of World War II that covered the city. A third letter gave Rosalie his impressions of the London trip, beginning with his original intention to go for a couple of days and staying a week instead. He described his thrill of seeing the old waterfront pubs and ships that brought memories of Whistler and Charles Dickens. He found beautiful clusters of yellow flowers amid the rubble from the bombings or half a building standing with rooms exposed, revealing the lives of people who had lived there. He recounted a sunny Sunday afternoon stroll, surrounded by red double-decker buses, peddlers hawking fruit, and girls in summer dresses, all in an air of gaiety. Suddenly he had heard a bang and turned to see a door swinging open and shut in the wind. He saw the wallpaper and a lopsided picture in a third-floor room and stopped to wonder about its seemingly apathetic occupant while all around him London throbbed with sunlight and life.

He noted the distinctions between monuments in Paris and those in London. The horses and people in the Parisian sculptures looked winged as if ready to fly away any minute, while the horses in English sculptures appeared to stubbornly refuse to move when the old colonels urged them along. He inferred that the rulers of the colonies, who commissioned the statues, had unwittingly portrayed the struggle of the rulers and the colonial people in the symbolism of the horses.

He found the people of London to be resilient after the terrific struggle with the Nazis and liked their description of their work as having "tidied up the place." He saw more physical evidence of reconstruction than he had found in Paris. Finding the British to have a "nice, jolly, jaunty spirit," he left with hopes of returning for a visit and, if his finances allowed, traveling to Italy as well.

When Jack returned to Paris, a representative from Lelong Perfumes, who came from New York to get publicity and materials, expressed interest in his work. After some time spent driving around Paris as the agent took on a tempera painting that Jack did on speculation and suggested subject matter that might be interesting to the company, Jack had second thoughts. He confided in Rosalie that the man ate up his time, and he had decided to confine his work to painting and would sell only on a definite basis. He added that, as he painted in the neighborhood, a French art critic passing by had congratulated him on his work.

Jack closed his letter, after sympathizing with his poor arm that had done all the writing and her almond eyes that had done all the reading, with the briefest of comments on her life, including congratulations on her salary increase, a note on his "not too comfortable" existence, along with missing the comforts of New York and friends, and casual questions about how she is doing. He did not mention her coming to Europe.

One day, Jack spotted a concierge with a long white mustache, wearing a beret, a striped collarless shirt, suspenders, and glasses. The mailman brought the doorman a stack of mail, which he checked through and discussed. Jack waited until they finished and the mailman departed before asking permission to paint the concierge.

The doorman read his newspaper while Jack painted. The cat came in, and Jack painted her, too. He was nearly finished when the man's wife came in dressed in her apron, broom in hand. She looked at the picture. "How about me? Why don't you paint me? I'll be at this window tomorrow."

The next day, the woman greeted him, "Bonjour, Mister Painter." She was dressed up with a gold brooch and her hat. No broom or apron.

"Young man, you look disappointed," she said.

"I wanted to paint a typical concierge."

"And what would they think of us in America? Start, please."

A discouraged Jack painted away.

Soon, he realized that his father, in his high school painting that caused the family trouble, and the concierge's wife were not the only people who wanted to dress up or to be portrayed in their best light. One summer day Jack spied a gendarme standing listlessly on duty at the French police station, its tricolor flag hanging motionless under the hot sun. He was nearly through painting him when the captain stepped out and came over to see what Jack was doing. "Mon Dieu! You can't paint him like that."

The captain turned to the gendarme. "Stand straight! You're being painted." The gendarme sucked in his stomach. The captain urged Jack to improve his painting with the new stance, but Jack said he was too late and began gathering his painting supplies, all the while listening to the captain scolding the policeman.

Jack shared his efforts with Roger, who worked in a textile factory and, like Jack, was always broke. Roger enjoyed Jack's candid painting and asked if he could accompany him on his artistic jaunts. On weekends he began to go with Jack, borrowing watercolors and paints. Jack kept his eyes open for art objects and for models, with high hopes that he would also see a beautiful girl when he went to a café with Roger and his friend Gaspard.

One Saturday, Roger borrowed Jack's supplies, and they headed to the Palais Royal. Jack painted a stooped little old lady carrying a net shopping bag full of food with a baguette sticking out of the top. She came around to see his painting. "Mmmmm. Très bon—very tasty, young man." She smacked her lips like she was tasting the colors and hobbled away. As they put their supplies up, Jack noticed that Roger had painted the older woman into his picture, too. During lunch at a nearby café, Roger made her lip-smacking sound. Jack looked up and saw a pretty girl coming toward them. The woman's noise became their signal of something good about to happen.

Jack rehearsed a scene in his head so he would be prepared if one of those pretty girls ever stopped to watch him paint. He'd say in French, "Do you like it?" and she'd say, "I do." Then he'd say, "Would you like to have some coffee or a drink with me?" and she'd say, "Yes, I would." In his daydream, he'd meet his true love in Paris. Instead, it seemed that the beautiful women came like flocks of birds just out of reach and took off when he approached.

❧

One afternoon, Jack heard the tinkle of bracelets as he toured the Musée Rodin. He turned and saw a blonde green-eyed girl in a light blue dress with tiny white daises viewing the exhibit with a friend. Jack thought the daisies looked like stars in a daytime sky. He followed them at a distance, moving in and out among the other patrons, watching her enjoy the sculptures and listening to her bell-like voice. The three of them met at the sculptured bronze head of Balzac.

"Do you speak English?" Jack asked.

"Yes, we do."

"Do you mind if I join you?"

She laughed softly. "Not at all," she said. "We feel like we sort of know you already." Perhaps he had not been as subtle as he thought in his shadowing. She said her name was Freddie. Jack forgot the friend's name as soon as she said it.

A bit chagrined, Jack asked, "Do you see *The Gates of Hell*?" They approached the doors, examining the swirling figures rising up on the green and gray patina. They studied *The Thinker*, brooding and silent. When the friends finished at the museum, Jack walked them to the metro. On the way, they told him they were Dutch students on the second day of a three-day holiday. Before they parted, Freddie agreed to meet Jack for lunch the following day.

Jack sketched the next day as he waited for Freddie at an outdoor café at Pont Neuf, enjoying the shimmering light on the falling autumn foliage. Perhaps he wanted to impress Freddie with his status as a Parisian artist. She slipped up behind him and studied his drawing. "How wonderful!" she said. "I'll keep it—to remember."

Jack suggested a picnic on the Seine River, and they stopped at a little shop for bread, cheese, sausage, and wine. They found a tree near the river and spread their lunch. Colorful leaves drifted down and little clouds drifted through the sky, while the sunlight glanced across the river as barges floated along.

After lunch, they wandered arm in arm to a nearby park. "Please sketch this," Freddie said. "It's too beautiful not to capture even a bit of it. One day, when you're sad, you'll look at it, and it'll make you happy again."

Jack drew a nearby boy into the picture. The boy came to look, and suddenly blew the whistle he wore around his neck. Jack jumped. He looked up as kids came from everywhere. "Put me in. Put me in. You put André in."

André stood close to Jack, blowing his whistle and directing the group. Jack tried to ignore them and draw while Freddie covered her ears.

Finally, Jack slammed down his notebook. "SCRAM!"

They stared in silence until one began to chant. "Chicago! Gangster! Chicago!" The other kids circled and joined the mantra.

Jack jumped toward them jabbing his fists in the air. "Beat it, you creeps!" The kids ran in all directions.

"My hero," Freddie said. "My American gangster."

Jack and Freddie relaxed again under the tree, sipping their wine while they watched the people. Nuns rode bicycles with their blue habits tucked under their sashes. Algerians tried to sell rugs until a policeman scared them off. A couple wearing matching sweaters and berets rode by on a bicycle built for two. A Black man and a white woman walked by, arm in arm.

"Ugh," Freddie said.

Jack looked at her, confused.

She leaned toward him and whispered, "Do you know that one Jew is as bad as ten Blacks?"

"What?"

"Yes," she said. "My parents have had much experience with these people. It's best to stay away from them if you know what's good for you."

"Let's go," Jack said.

"Where to?"

"Let's just go."

They started walking. Jack felt like their wires had disconnected and the world had disappeared behind a thick wall of glass. Caught up in his own thoughts, he knew he should speak up. He reasoned in his head. *Tell her now. Tell her you're a Jew. Don't sound too flustered or too upset. Be on top of it. Be proud.*

"What's happened?" she asked. "Everything's changed. You're so sad."

"I was just thinking."

They walked on in silence. "If you don't become that happy American gangster again, I think I'm going to cry." She looked serious. Jack knew he should set her straight, but he couldn't think how. He kept walking.

"I think I'd best go home," Freddie said. "I'm suddenly so tired and very sad."

Jack decided he'd tell her when he said good-bye at the metro, but when she hurried down the steps and called back to remind him of their farewell supper before her midnight train, he still didn't say anything. When she had gone, he went to the post office and sent a note by a pneumatic tube.

Dear Freddie,

I won't be meeting you tonight. I'll spare you further contamination. You see, I'm a member of one of those peoples your parents want to save you from—one of those Jews . . .

He finished the note and walked out, knowing she would get it in a couple of hours. He walked and walked. The streets seemed to be full of lovers walking arm in arm. He went into a movie house and saw *The Wizard of Oz*—twice. It made him homesick.

When he came out, it was dark and chilly. He stopped for a ham sandwich and coffee and wandered some more.

When he finally returned to Pension Jeanne, the landlady said, "A young lady, a blonde, has been after you all night. She came here three times—three times." She handed him an envelope. "She left this for you. You men. Where have you been? The poor thing looked so upset."

Jack opened the envelope. The note said: "... I'm the worst and rudest person in the world. But please don't take everything that I'm saying for granted, because I'm but a very dumb and young girl who says exactly what enters into her head.... Please forgive me, and don't be so foolish. Love, Frederique."

He did not see her again.

Roger and Jack became wanderers as they took the metro or autobus around the city, looking for unsuspecting subjects for their next paintings. One afternoon, full of anticipation for what they could find, Roger suddenly froze. When Jack asked if he was all right, he couldn't answer at first but stood staring at the large building with a shiny aluminum dome. Finally, Roger found his voice and explained that they were facing the Velodrome where police had rounded up the Jews for the Nazis, even bringing in children, although the Germans had not asked for them. The Jeanne family had saved him by hiding him in a barrel in their attic when his parents were taken with all the others to the gas chambers in Germany. As Jack led him away, he added that the place was also known as the Palais des Sports.

Jack's fourth letter to Rosalie took a negative tone, evidently as she continued to make suggestions that she might come to Europe. He complained of a summer cold that made her phone call unclear and caused his writing to be brief because of the difficulty of focusing his eyes. He made a list including how he missed her, the unpleasant experience it would be for her to live in Paris under the present conditions, his plan to go to Italy with the probability of being back to New York in December, and the unreasonable risk to her job. He concluded with nostalgia for the good times they had and a forewarning that he would be out in the country for several days if he felt well enough, so she should not expect to hear from him again soon.

A cable had come from his friend Jay Williams, who was traveling with his wife Barbara and six-year-old son Christopher, asking him to look for a modest inexpensive pension they could rent for about a week. Jack made reservations for them at his own, claiming it was as good as any and had the advantage of being close to Boulevard du Montparnasse. Jay recounted that experience in *A Climate of Change*, published in 1956 with Jack's illustrations.

Jay's description of the pension was even worse than Jack's, beginning with the food. Barbara had gone to school in Paris when she was eleven or twelve, and her descriptions of the cuisine had Jay drooling in anticipation. Yet, he described the first meal as a strange grayish-brown object in a small puddle of congealed gravy, accompanied by potatoes and a collection of cuttings from an old wet piece of cardboard. Their assumption that things would be better at the next meal was met with what he described as "grease soup, filet of grease, and although this may seem impossible, a kind of greasy fruit salad." To their astonishment, Jack appeared to eat with good appetite as if there was nothing out of the ordinary. Their pain eased somewhat when they found a small inexpensive restaurant where they splurged once a day for a good meal. Sleep deprivation came from nearby church bells that rang every hour, rattling the windows and exploding like a thunderstorm. The Williams family did enjoy walks in the gardens, bus rides, and meeting Jack's friends, including Roger, but the highlight of the trip was the three days in the country that Jack had mentioned to Rosalie. The group wandered the countryside, ate stewed rabbit, and picnicked in the meadows.

Jack's fifth letter to Rosalie reported on the refreshing trip and hiking in nature with Jay. Dialing back from his previous letter, Jack encouraged Rosalie to come to Europe if she could come at no expense to herself and if it would improve her position. He thought it would be great if she could see another part of the world with him and added that he planned to spend most of his time in Florence. He cautioned that while he looked forward to seeing her, it would be too soon to make plans for their future, but they must wait until they got together to let things take a natural and relaxed course. He encouraged her to acknowledge that this plan was but a paraphrase of what she had been saying in her letters.

His sixth letter gave a halfhearted apology for the cool letter he had written previously, claiming the excuse of having been in a bad mood and offering as proof his actions of applying for return passage for both of them in November at a rate that would not cost her company too much. He also proposed a trip that would cost them no more than $150 each for the month or so that she planned to be in Europe. Beginning in Paris and its surroundings, they could travel to southern France, Italy, Rome, Milan, Florence, Venice, and back through Switzerland with England and Scotland as possibilities if there was time.

Sandwiched in this trip plan, yet another brief cautionary paragraph warned, "We could not at this point make very specific predictions about future development together, so there must have been certain elements that needed resolving, since if this were not so, we would be together now." He went on to say how much he looked forward to sharing the good things with her that would help avoid the troublesome. After saying how much he missed her, he hoped she could accept the experience for what it was worth and wait to see what followed.

He ended this letter with a description of his frustration with trying to find customers for his work in France. One account thought his work innovative and unlike anything they had in France, while Jack saw himself as highly influenced by French painters. Some were difficult to work with, others paid poorly, and he cited some unnamed European traditions, which he thought, "They would do well without."

His goal when he returned to the United States was to develop his own style rather than confining himself to his tradition. He claimed not to be worried about finding new work or finding living and studio space but would cross that bridge when he came to it.

After commenting on the many things he had learned from living in the culture as well as the museums, he apologized for making her read his handwriting in the long letter. He closed with anticipation of her arrival in late September or early October while still urging caution that she not jeopardize her job.

The end of August brought letters making final plans. His schedule demanded that he not leave Paris before the first of October in order to receive his VA check. He proposed that she plan her itinerary to arrive on the second or third, giving him time to arrange for an inexpensive room for them to share and a chance to meet her at the station on her arrival. He posited several choices for her return, the travel back together on a ship apparently abandoned, and signed off one of the letters with a hopeful "I've been champing at the bit and hoping for the best— so try to work it out if you can."

An undated letter to Rosalie that apparently fits in this time frame began to coordinate plans for her trip. Jack suggested that she take her vacation the last week in October and three weeks in November. This was in part a business trip for Rosalie since he suggested the boat fare would save her company more than a hundred dollars. He enclosed forms for her to fill out with a request that she would let him know where she planned to stay in Milan so he could work it out to spend his time with her there.

In the next letter, he asked if she got the forms and requested that she send him three tubes of Permanent Green in "Martini" tempera paints. He sent love to her and to New York.

Their trip to Italy exceeded Jack's greatest expectations. Rosalie's cosmetics company paid for a suite at a deluxe hotel in Milan. They felt like they were in a movie come to life with gracious service, gourmet food, and fine wines, with a bed that could sleep four and a huge marble bathtub. Jack attended fashion shows in palazzos with Rosalie and had meals with Italian representatives of the fashion scene. At dinner, they mentioned their delight in the local wines to their companion, which led to an invitation for a vineyard tour.

As his practice had been since childhood, Jack took in the early morning scenery on their sightseeing visit. The scene reminded him of Jean-Baptiste-Camille Corot's early Italian landscapes with a sprawling vineyard amid monastery-topped hills filled with dark green cypress trees. Their hosts were a mother, referred to as the "Old Contessa" and her daughter, descendants of Machiavelli. The Old Contessa took them to Machiavelli's farmhouse, a monastic cell in a one-story plaster building with one high window, necessitating a step up to look out on the landscape of Tuscany. She said this had been where Machiavelli spent his life, thinking, working, and writing *The Prince*.

In his mind, Jack compared these current residents with a large family of children he might have known in his childhood tenements. Long garlands of garlic hung from the ceilings with pots and pans hanging from the walls and an old-fashioned cooking stove in the corner. Outside, clothing hung from lines to dry just as he remembered from his youth in Brooklyn.

Preparing to leave, their guide plucked a yellow chrysanthemum, bowed gallantly and presented it to the Old Contessa and handed Jack and Rosalie over to the English-speaking German overseer with his lederhosen and Tyrolean hat to continue the tour.

They watched the grape picking. They passed a woman on a ladder propped against a tree, dropping fruit into a basket suspended from a branch. As she worked, she told a story to the little girl sitting against the trunk of the tree, picking petals off a daisy. Large women with red-stained feet and rolled up skirts smashed grapes in enormous vats. White oxen wearing red and purple tassels to ward off flies and evil spirits brought carts laden with grapes. Jack sketched and painted all morning until the tolling monastery bells sang out at noon.

The Contessa had become busy and forgotten the arrangements she was to have made for lunch. Jack and Rosalie watched the grape workers arrange themselves in a circle and set out their food. A man with a white head of hair, bushy eyebrows, and moustache came over to them, bowed, and grinned showing his two teeth. Pointing toward the bells and then to his stomach and then to theirs, he murmured, "Mmmm," and began chewing motions. Jack caught on that they were being invited to eat, and he and Rosalie joined in the circle sitting on the grass, but that would not do. Quickly, the group indicated they were not to sit on the ground but on the two wooden crates that had been brought for them.

The group watched as Jack and Rosalie tasted the shared meal of a spicy tomato and potato stew, slices of hard salami, big chunks of bread, and wine. They smiled and began to eat, offering seconds to their guests. Jack saw how little they had, yet how much they wanted to please, and signed with his forefinger that he would have just a little bit more. He looked over and saw the little girl Gabriella fast asleep against Rosalie, tired out from her daisy picking.

Soon after the vineyard workers returned to their task, they met the overseer, who apologized for the lunch, but Jack assured him that all was well. By late afternoon, Jack completed his sketches, and they began taking leave of their hosts. The Contessa wished him luck, and the overseer drove them back in a jeep along a road lined with the vineyard workers, who gave them grapes and clusters of flowers about every ten feet. Gabriella's mother held her high as they waved good-bye.

The doorman at the hotel was startled when they drove up and reeled into the lobby, dust covered and laden with their gifts followed by flies buzzing in pursuit. With no air-conditioning, more flies joined in such abundance that they telephoned the desk to ask for help.

Rosalie's next assignment was Rome, where they had a nice hotel again. They excused themselves from business when they could and wandered the streets and ate at the small bistros. One afternoon as Jack watched the erection of a huge Coca-Cola sign above the city, he said in English to a man nearby that they were getting one of our major achievements. The man answered in near perfect English that he had thought it might have come from outer space. As they visited over glasses of wine, Jack explained that he was an American artist, working in Paris. The man was Lionello Torossi, a public relations person from a film studio and a friend of many of the great Italian artists and actors. As a consequence of making this acquaintance, Jack and Rosalie were introduced to the entertainers and invited to many homes for dinner, where people spoke barely a word of English, but they had the best of times just the same.

When Rosalie returned to the United States, Jack became overwhelmed with homesickness and loneliness. A few days later, Lionello brought an invitation that he guaranteed would cheer Jack up. There was to be an exhibition with a few people invited to an opening if he would like to come. He finished with the high point. Pablo Picasso would be there.

The next evening, guests chattered softly, until all heads turned toward the opening door when Picasso entered. Jack would have vivid memories of what he saw. Picasso's head reminded him of the artist's sculptured skulls, with large black penetrating eyes fixed directly on Jack as he shook his hand in a strong handshake. Jack would not remember their conversation, but he spent the rest of the evening following Picasso out of the corners of his eyes as discreetly as he could. Like many people before him, he was taken with the painter's eyes and watched his head move this way and that like a beacon in a lighthouse.

When Jack returned to Paris feeling dislocated and hungering for conversation in English, he decided to act on an invitation he had received in Milan from a British men's fashion designer. Jack had mentioned that he had done illustrations for *Menswear* magazine. The designer was working on a similar article and invited him to come to London, asking if Jack had an interest in illustrating the piece. Jack contacted the publisher, who urged him to come right away if he was interested.

Self-conscious about what he saw as his worn clothes when he was in Milan, Jack thought the event called for a new suit. Roger knew a place that was cheap and stylish. They entered the dimly lit basement shop, looking for a dark charcoal gray suit.

The first one the salesman brought out seemed dull and lifeless. Roger translated Jack's concern to the salesman, whose face lit up. He had the very thing. He brought out a suit with a bluish-gray tinge with a slightly stronger pinstripe. Jack tried it on and found a perfect fit, and the price was right. They congratulated each other on their find all the way home, and Roger helped him pack for his trip.

Jack arrived in London late the next afternoon with his appointment for 7:30 that night, unpacked his suit, and started to hang it up. Some mistake must have been made. In daylight, the suit was dark purple with terrible bold stripes, and he had brought nothing else suitable to wear.

It was still quite light when Jack made his appearance. Three impeccably dressed men standing at the bar stopped talking. Jack felt like a neon sign flashing off and on as the men could not hide their astonishment, though they treated him with courtesy. He tried to carry on a conversation, hoping night would fall soon with only amber lighting, yet the sun lingered in the sky. They invited him to the terrace, overlooking the Thames. Eventually, twilight came, softening the shapes and colors in the harbor and in his suit. Relaxing in the good company, he entertained his new companions with the story of his purple suit.

In the morning at his hotel, Jack asked for scrambled eggs for breakfast. The waiter said the cook would be glad to prepare them if he could only find some eggs, but the aftermath of the war left fresh foods in short supply.

In the comfort of English speakers again, Jack wandered the streets. Bombed-out holes formed entire blocks with cross-sections of sliced away buildings and heaps of rubble everywhere. In spite of all the destruction and shortages, Jack felt energy in the air. Londoners hurried to work on red double-decker buses or the subway, wearing their bowlers and carrying tightly wrapped umbrellas, and he thought he could feel a sense of victory and hope for better times. He asked a woman for directions. She broke into a smile and said, "You're a Yank [American], aren't you? We've had a lot of you lads here—good chaps," expressing a sentiment he found common during his stay in England.

He returned to Paris on 1 November and back to the United States on 10 November. Once again, he faced his old problems of staying healthy, avoiding loneliness, and earning a living. He'd recovered his love of painting, but he needed to buy food and pay rent. Maybe he could do commercial art or teach. Maybe he could make a deal with a landlord.

Back in New York once again, Jack felt alone. His relationship with Rosalie had faded, the first in a series of liaisons that would last for a while and then come to an end, though the friendship might remain. He received an envelope from Rosalie returning his letters in January, 1950 with a cover letter saying, "Dear Jack, You asked me for these several weeks ago, and they were mailed. . . . They were returned as 'addressee unknown.' I guess the Christmas scramble did it."

Her name would show up in the dedication for *The Snowy Day*, and a final Rosalie letter in 1982 in his correspondence collection reveals old friends catching up on lost time.

In an interview in his later life, he analyzed the pattern he set for himself and realized that he had followed his mother's advice. She had told him not to get married but just buy girls gifts and have affairs. She also advised against having children. Whether this advice or a fear of long-term commitment was his reason is subject to speculation. He certainly grew up seeing an unhappy marriage as the one he knew best.

CHAPTER 8

STARVING ARTIST?

KEATS WOULD LATER REFER TO HIS NEXT FEW YEARS AS A BIG sleep. His old struggles with finances, health, and relationships seemed to have been held in abeyance for his return. He saw his work in this period as derivative rather than springing from his creativity. His disorganized search for himself continued.

Landlords learned that artists, writers, and actors who needed low-rent apartments improved them while they waited for jobs so they could pay the rent, but when the artists ran behind in their payments, they still received an eviction notice. The landlord wanted more than improvement to his property. As Jack walked home, he might hear a shout from a neighbor, "Brace yourself, Keats! There's another greetin' for ya." He'd find a sign in Old English type on his door: "NOTICE OF EVICTION." Jack would tear the notice into tiny bits, throw it into the air like confetti, wave at the neighbor, and find another apartment.

One night, Jack arrived to visit friends before they got home and happened to meet Mira, who was babysitting the friends' children. She had an abusive husband who had shared her experience of fleeing from the Holocaust. Jack began dropping in at his friends' house to visit when Mira babysat. When she separated from her husband, she and Jack moved in together in a walk-down, a few steps below street level. Jack caulked and sanded the floors, plastered and painted the flaking walls, sowed grass in the backyard and sealed the windows. Mira became a casserole expert, creating dishes from fish heads, organ parts, rice, tomato sauce, and vegetables, which they paired with day-old bread and cheap wine. In the evening, they recounted the events of their days, read to each other at bedtime, and tried to outwit the mosquitoes. In the darkness, they lured those pests, attracted by the smell of the garbage cans outside the window, to the light of a flashlight and snatched them with their fists. After the boon of a well-paying assignment, they bought window screens, which left them with only the odor of the garbage.

The two were relieved when Mira's husband agreed to a divorce, and they began to make friends with their neighbors, including the artist Henry Koerner, who was beginning to make a name for himself in the art world with a feature in *Newsweek* magazine.

Slowly and with some help from his friends, Jack began to make deals in a hodgepodge of places for his art and illustrations while Mira picked up babysitting jobs. The National Academy accepted Jack's gouache of Place Saint-Michel for a show. The Associated American Artists Gallery hung more of his paintings, with an ad featuring "the Plaza" in their brochure below a signed lithograph with a quotation from Jack: "Typical of the unexpected and dramatic contrasts of New York City is the phenomenon of the Plaza. Here one finds the serenity and quietude of the Hansom carriages, trees, pigeons and the fountain. Behind loom tall gray buildings. I was particularly moved by the first snow of winter." The brochure went on to note his love of painting cities, especially Paris, London, and New York, and the prominence he had achieved as a water-colorist, mural painter, illustrator, and teacher. In the brochure photograph, he examined the first proof of "the Plaza."

Response to the showing surprised Jack. The gallery called to say someone wanted to buy three of the paintings from the French Lines window display.

"Those three?"

"You don't sound happy, Keats. Something wrong? We're selling them at the price you asked for."

"Ahhh, well—they're sort of my favorites."

Silence.

Then the voice came again. "There is something I should apprise you of, and I hope it doesn't come as too great a blow—but we're in the business to sell paintings. Call me tomorrow morning and let me know how this suits you." Jack needed the money and let them sell his beloved paintings.

When the check arrived, Jack threw a backyard party for his assorted friends and neighbors. On benches around a picnic table, they feasted on watermelon, corn on the cob, and cheap wine. Gerome, a beginning dress designer, gave Mira a new dress for the occasion that she had modeled for him as he created the prototype. Sylvie, who shyly fed morsels to her husband, mingled with Freddy, a nine-year-old Puerto Rican who would one day star in a Keats book, and with the Johnsons, a family from across the street who ran a café. Ici, a tank corpsman, told stories of the Battle of the Bulge. Bennie Parolo thought he'd found a valuable painting in the garbage and asked Jack if he'd look at it tomorrow. Henry Koerner sang Pagliacci's aria with gusto. In the background, they heard Mrs. Grant sing from across the way with a voice that had them wondering if she was in trouble and needed the police.

The next day, Jack met Bennie to look at his discovery. In his new business, Bennie scoured the neighborhood for discarded treasures, cleaned them up, and sold them to an antique shop. With an uncanny eye for value and an outgoing personality, he soon appeared in flea markets under the name Parolo Enterprises. In the new find, Jack saw a two- by three-foot painting with a flaked off corner, revealing a discolored canvas with a faint unreadable signature. Under the dirt was a quiet landscape with a female nude. Thinking it might be the work of an early Expressionist or a competent student, he offered to take Bennie to the Lilienfeld Gallery.

An excited Bennie researched in art books to find out what he was holding and discovered similarities to Munch paintings. Bennie and Jack were an eager pair until the morning of the appointment at the Lilienfeld. Jack smelled something, linseed oil or varnish, coming from the bag Bennie held. Bennie drew out the painting with the flaked corner covered with fresh paint. He praised another friend who had cleaned and varnished the painting to perfection.

Jack did what he could to remove the paint, but it remained shiny and sticky. Reluctantly, he entered the gallery with Bennie and his treasure in a paper bag. Dr. Lilienfeld took the painting, sniffed the air, and touched the sticky canvas, with Mrs. Lilienfeld peering over his shoulder. He smiled gently as he looked back and forth between Jack and Bennie. "Gentlemen," he said. "I don't think there is much to say about the—painting." His wife closed her eyes and shook her head.

As they left, Bennie pointed out other galleries and suggested that they might retouch the painting into a new color that was not quite so bright. This time Jack closed his eyes and shook his head.

In the meantime, Itch pursued science and worked in a research laboratory, making a name for himself as Dr. Martin Pope. He and Lillie tried to support Jack's sales. Lillie showed some of his French sketches and watercolors to her friends, even a few that she rescued from his wastebasket, and sold several paintings. Usually they sold them for three to thirty-five dollars, but one sold for seventy-five dollars. Jack also painted some note cards with good sales.

The Freedmans, still friends with Jack from his high school years when she was his English teacher, had a custom of sending an annual family newsletter with their holiday greetings and asked Jack to make drawings to illustrate them.

Even with help from his friends, worries over finances and his health dogged him. After a fight with Mira, he complained to his doctor about sleepless nights. The doctor prescribed Seconal. After the couple's next fight, with the help of the medication, he fell asleep before she did. First, he took the pills occasionally and then more often until he eventually never traveled without them. He knew the danger of mixing them with alcohol and disciplined himself to take them three hours after and eight hours before drinking. He visited different doctors to renew his prescription and refused to go back to the one who would not renew it without a checkup. All the time, he believed that none of his friends knew of his habit.

Bit by bit, Jack began to make a few sales outside his friendship circle. The I. Miller Shoe Store exhibited one of his murals. Paul and Louise Cleland from Morehead City, North Carolina, were attracted to it as they walked down Fifth Avenue. When they went in to inquire about it, the store manager put them in touch with Jack. They bought one of his large paintings of a tropical scene in the Virgin Islands. Mr. Cleland wrote a letter to Jack when the painting arrived at their home. He said it fit in nicely and added just the colors they wanted in their home. He promised to recommend Jack's painting to others and invited him to visit if he ever came to Morehead City.

Slowly Jack was given commissions to paint covers and do illustrations for magazines—*Reader's Digest, Collier's,* and

Playboy. He illustrated for an advertising magazine called *Texaco's People* from the oil company. Jack's income grew, but he worried that his good fortune might not last.

Mira read manuscripts with him and discussed colors that would capture the mood of the story. One evening they discussed a manuscript jacket assignment by V. Sackville West for a book called *The Easter Party*. Mira went to sleep at the far end of the room away from the noises of the street. There were no phone calls, no errands—just the light he had turned on over his drawing table near the window. In an almost hypnotic stare, Jack began to apply wash after wash of color. Slowly the picture he wanted appeared. Tall dark green trees emerged against a violet-pink sky. When he finished the painting, Jack looked out and saw dawn lighting the city. He'd forgotten to go to bed. The last time he'd looked, the world was pitch black. He did not realize that something like the dawn was also rising in his life.

After *The Easter Party* was published, Elizabeth Riley, a children's book editor at Crowell Publishers, spotted the jacket cover as she walked past the Doubleday bookstore. Attracted by the illustration, she turned into the store to find the name of the artist. She gave Keats a call to see if he was willing to illustrate a juvenile book with a similar mood.

The book jacket was for *Step to the Music* by Phyllis Whitney, who was becoming well known for her children's and adults' mysteries. Since the book was set on Staten Island, where Mrs. Whitney lived, Jack traveled on the ferry from Brooklyn over the Verrazano Narrows to see the island. He wanted to be sure he drew his pictures right. The layout for the two books has a kinship, like siblings but not identical twins. *The Easter Party* cover shows a man and his dog looking down on a scene of a country estate framed by trees in full leaf on either side. *Step to the Music* has a couple observing a ship sailing down the river framed by trees bare of their foliage. Similar wash tones of color created both.

Ms. Riley liked the book cover for *Step to the Music* and asked Jack if he would be interested in illustrating a children's book about a traveling "nurse on horseback" in the Smoky Mountains, who treated both people and animals in remote areas of Appalachia. Jack felt a need to do justice to the children who would read it, but what did a man who grew up in Brooklyn know about Appalachia? Once again, he decided to see life there for himself. He and Mira would travel to the Smokies.

Jack recalled an Army acquaintance from Tennessee. Traveling there would give him a sense of setting. Leaving Mira in the hotel the first morning, he hitched a ride on the back of an ice truck. "Where you going?" the iceman asked.

"I don't know," said Jack. "I'll just tap on the window when I want to get off." Holding his art supplies tightly as they bounced along the bumpy, curving road, he gazed at the mountain landscape and wondered if he would find what he was looking for. Around the next curve, hanging on the mountain, Jack spotted a rickety wooden shack with a rusty corrugated tin roof and a stone chimney. He pounded on the window to be let off.

Jack settled down to draw across the dusty road from the cabin as chickens strutted in and out of the house. A little girl sat on the steps with her corncob doll. She inched over until she was in the middle of the scene, and Jack added her to the picture.

Finished with his sketch, Jack crossed the road and walked up to the house. When he greeted her, the little girl said her name was Judy. "Do you know what I was doing?" Jack asked.

"Yes," she said. "You were drawing me."

"Has anybody ever drawn you before?"

"No."

"Would you like to see?"

"Yes."

Judy's mother, Elizabeth McCain, came out on the porch. Jack explained he was an artist, drawing pictures for a book about a native of the Smokies. She said that Pa and Grandpa would soon be in for lunch and invited him to join them.

At lunch, upon learning that Jack was staying in town at the Hotel Wrigley, Robert McCain said that was too far to travel daily and invited him to stay with them. Jack explained that Mira was with him, calling her his wife. Robert assured him that was no trouble. When Jack offered to pay for any extra expense, Robert replied, "Then the deal's off."

Jack realized he'd hurt Robert's pride and backed off. "No, no, I accept. I'll be back tomorrow."

The next morning, Robert and Grandpa McCain were already working in the fields when Jack and Mira arrived. Elizabeth took them on a tour of the farm, explaining it was tobacco harvest season. Their living came from the three hundred dollars they hoped to get from the tobacco harvest, supplemented by the men's hunting expeditions. The little group passed the barn where the tobacco would be hung. A cold stream flowed around a milk jug, a cow grazed in the fields, and a pig waddled by. Vegetables grew on the steep rocky slopes.

They met Robert up the road. He cautioned Jack not to stray more than two miles from the house for sketching lest one of the local moonshiners mistake him for a "revenuer" and shoot him before he could say, "I am an artist." A neighbor came along to plan the next day's harvest. Community farmers pitched in to help each other cut, gather, and hang the tobacco for drying. The next day was the McCain's day.

When they reached the bottom of the hill, Elizabeth filled big buckets of water to haul up to the house. Jack offered to take them, but she frowned. "This here's woman's work."

After supper as they sat on the porch, Jack watched the red sun sink behind the Smokies. Colors shifted from blues to violets and purples. Gray mists rose and a wisp of smoke curled toward the sky. Slowly, night fell with starry skies and the songs of crickets and frogs.

Jack and Mira slept well deep in the soft goose down mattress and woke at dawn to sounds of a crowing rooster, barking dogs, and bustling preparations for the day. They smelled coffee and frying bacon. Dressing quickly, they joined the family for coffee, grits, and apples fried with bacon—a breakfast Jack found to be unusual and sensational.

Mira helped Elizabeth and Judy in the kitchen while Jack carried in sacks of vegetables and lent a hand to set up tables and chairs outside, brought in by the neighbors for the lunchtime meal. Finished with his assigned chores, Jack sketched men, women, and children moving through the fields cutting the tobacco, stacking it in mule-drawn carts to carry to the barn, and hanging it in the rafters to dry. At noon, the neighbors sat at the long table layout filled with fresh vegetables, said grace, ate their lunch, and returned to work.

A few nights later, the neighbors gathered for an end of harvest celebration. A family provided the music as the grandfather played the fiddle and called the square dance, the father plucked the banjo, and the son squeezed the accordion. Old people sat around the walls tapping their feet to keep time. A woman danced in the center, her body loose like a puppet. She went faster and faster. Others joined her until the cracking of shoes on the floor made a wild noise. His grinning new friends slapped Jack on the back and invited him and Mira to join in when the fiddler called out, "Take your partners. Do-si-do." Jack thought they danced quite well.

The next day, when they had to leave, Judy wept uncontrollably. Jack and Mira assured her they would try to return. They promised to write letters and to send a copy of the book when it was finished.

The promise to stay in touch would be partially kept, proven by two letters Jack saved that were addressed to "Mr. and Mrs. Jack Keats." The first, dated 31 December 1953, thanked them for the gifts they had sent to each of the McCains. Elizabeth asked about his book and Mira's schoolwork and shared the news that Judy had her tonsils out.

The second, dated 9 November 1954, thanked Jack and Mira for sending the book, with the comment that the pictures looked familiar, especially the kitchen. Perhaps there were no more exchanges because life with Jack and Mira had taken a turn by the time the second letter arrived.

Returning home from the mountains to what seemed like another world in New York City, Jack saw the paper on the door: "NOTICE OF EVICTION." But there was also good news in his mailbox. He had been accepted as an instructor at a famous correspondence school for artists in Connecticut. They agreed to an arrangement by which he worked Mondays through Wednesdays including nights, giving him the equivalent of a week's work and pay, with the other four days left free for him to be at home in the city and freelance. Mira got a job in a Hungarian food shop in Manhattan. With a few days before their jobs started, they spent some time in museums and making plans for the future since they would both be employed. Nevertheless, Jack sensed that Mira was becoming distracted and distant.

A warm welcome awaited Jack on his first Monday at the new job. His school had textbooks with lessons, diagrams, and reproductions of illustrations, giving him the idea that he might learn something new himself. In his orientation, they told him the school's purpose was to reach out to people who couldn't afford college and university art courses or were too far away to take advantage of them. Top illustrators would come by and visit every month or so. Influenced by his own past as a poor and struggling artist and with his altruism, he was pleased to be able to help these would-be artists as well as get a steady income for himself.

The company introduced him to teaching by the numbers. When he examined the work his students submitted, he was required to consult a chart of standard paragraphs and read into a Dictaphone, "Dear Miss Sylvester, 1, 3, 8, and so forth . . ." The machine informed the typists, who typed the paragraphs into a personal letter.

Jack was quickly disappointed because of the minimal standards of the school. Only occasionally did they drop an unskilled student and refund their money. Most disheartened students dropped out on their own, leaving the company to profit since payment for the course had been required at the start.

As time passed, sometimes his students explained that a lesson was late because of family problems or asked a technical question. Jack added a short note on the end of his numbered answers. "I do hope your mother recovers speedily. Sincerely, E. J. Keats." The typists working from the Dictaphone complained when his notes made them fall behind in their quotas. He soon received a Memo to Keats: "Cut the bleeding-heart act. Stick to the lessons."

The pitch by the salesmen bothered Jack even more than the automatic lessons. They made people believe they had talent and could be trained by famous illustrators. Jack looked at the samples sent in by prospective students and thought some of them looked like they'd been painted with brooms.

At home, his weekends passed civilly but with an undercurrent of tension with Mira. With the strange work schedule, the frustrations of his job, and the anxiety with Mira, he got additional prescriptions for Seconal to help him sleep. The pills gave him a high that produced a talking jag, and he phoned friends and told stories for lengthy periods of time. At work, he dozed through briefings. Since he had a quota to meet, he added uppers for daytime. Doctors prescribed in abundant numbers, and he rotated among several to put a respectable time between prescriptions. The tension with Mira and dependence on Seconal left him drained when he got up on Mondays at five-thirty to take the subway to Grand Central Station, the train to Connecticut, and the bus to the school. Since black coffee was not sufficient, he added an upper or two, which produced a fuzzy inaudible voice for the lessons.

Jack began to be suspicious of what Mira did in his absence and called home periodically to find her always there, yet the tension between them increased. Mira began to question how many Seconals he took, telling him she knew because his irises became enlarged and he talked strangely. Trying to drum up work, he visited publishers and regaled them with jokes and stories until he heard they thought he was taking up too much of their time and wanted him to deliver his samples and leave.

Before long, out of a job and his relationship with Mira over, self-doubt overtook Jack. He picked up embarrassing lackluster jobs, worked during the day, took the bus home, and popped a Seconal on the way to the house. He didn't think he was an addict, but for a time he lived a life of fuzziness and self-delusion. One night he came home and opened his big closet with its arrangement of inks. Picking up a bottle that had no liquid, he shook it and a tiny bit of dried pigment bounced around, sounding to him like a death rattle. In it, he saw a metaphor of what he was doing to himself.

Likely giving motivation to restore his resolve, regular assignments for book jackets began to come in, including a book jacket
and an illustration featuring Silas Marner, his old fictional friend
from high school. Jack illustrated an entire reading textbook
called *Panorama* published by Scott, Foresman and Company
in 1957, both the student edition and the teacher's manual. He
picked up commercial assignments from Allstate Life Insurance
and Texaco. He continued painting jacket covers for adult books
and drawing illustrations for magazines like *Collier's*, *Esquire*, and
Playboy. He painted several covers for *Reader's Digest*.

Jubilant for Sure, the Appalachian book, was selected as one
of the fifty best-illustrated books of the year. Phyllis Whitney
liked his work on *Step to the Music*, so she requested that he be
the cover artist for *Mystery on the Isle of Skye*. This one was set
in Scotland. Of course, Jack needed to travel to Scotland to be
sure he drew the pictures right. He became friends with Phyllis
and her husband and visited them several times on Staten Island.
She found him to be a gentle, humorous man with a quick wit
and interesting conversation. She began to request him as the
illustrator for her adult book jackets. Between 1953 and 1960, he
painted jackets for nine of her books. That same year, Jack took
a trip to Cuba to be sure his illustrations were right for *Three
Young Kings*. The little boy who grew up in Brooklyn tenements
was becoming quite a world traveler.

After his success with *Jubilant for Sure*, Jack received more
and more calls to illustrate children's books. During the next ten
years, he illustrated more than fifty books for other authors. He
used pens, pencils, or charcoal with a touch of color for most of
these illustrations. Two things nagged his mind as he drew and
painted these pictures for children's books. The stories seemed
rigid. He wanted to feel something happening in a child's life.
The second problem was the lack of diversity in books. Children

from many cultures had populated his childhood neighborhood, and now he saw them on the streets outside his window. Why weren't they in books?

Even with the eviction notices of the past behind him and much success, Jack remained uneasy. Would he continue to get assignments? Would he get more painting jobs? Would he get enough to disprove his father's prediction that he would starve? Jack might not have been so worried if he could have seen a short distance into his future. An answer to his anxiety and his dissatisfaction with the books he illustrated came quite by surprise.

Jack joined with Pat Cherr to write the kind of children's book he wanted. His former nine-year-old Puerto Rican neighbor Freddy became his model for Juanito, the book's hero. In *My Dog Is Lost*, Juanito, who speaks only Spanish, loses his dog Pepito. Jack's art used heavy lead pencil and a single red color separation, just right for the dog's rojo color, red brick walls, and excited phrases. He did not need a trip to know Juanito's surroundings. Juanito walks the streets from Jack's childhood memory bank in a city setting that was seldom portrayed in children's books at that time. After Juanito gets a bank teller to make him a sign in English, "My dog is lost," he enlists children from the neighborhoods of Chinatown, Harlem, Little Italy, and Park Avenue to help him search for his pet. Hand-signaled language gives them the description of his dog, and the kids become new friends in their successful search. The book fulfilled Jack's desire to include children of many cultures taking part in a happening in their lives. *My Dog Is Lost* was just the beginning. He would claim his next venture as the one in which he woke up from his deep sleep and found himself.

$\mathcal{A}$ Story in the Snow

ONE NIGHT, A WALK OUT INTO THE FALLING SNOW TRIGGERED memories for Jack and a few of his friends. Jack thought what looked like white silent manna fell from heaven as they reminisced about their childhood excitement. Swinging their arms and legs as they lay on their backs, they made snow angels. Dragging their feet and sticks through the freshly fallen snow, they designed patterns. They built fortresses and stockpiled snowballs, sometimes packed so hard they stung and sometimes so soft they fell apart like powder. They remembered eating the snow, jumping and rolling in it, and snowball fights. An excited Jack thought he could write a children's book about these remembrances. "If I do," he said, "I'll dedicate it to you guys."

Jack embarked on an experience that night that would open a door in children's literature and would turn his own life around. Jack found his hero waiting in his studio. He pulled out the clipping of the little boy being checked for malaria, saved from *Life* magazine, that had rotated between his studio walls and his desk drawer and put it right above his drawing table. This was his book, and he could choose the protagonist.

The manuscripts he'd illustrated occasionally had a Black child in the background, but none featured a Black child. The entire text he had done for *Panorama* had no Black children, and even the students illustrated in the teacher's guide entering class were middle class and white. Now he could choose. He placed the child he thought should have been there all along in the center of his story, and his hero would have a happening, an experience.

Jack had come to love this little boy that he would call Peter, but Peter must become real. He studied Black children and made many sketches in order for Peter to be in the book as himself, not as a white child colored brown. He wanted Black kids and white kids to like Peter, but more than that, he wanted them to know that Peter was there.

His art, as well as the action of his story, reached back into his own childhood. Jack thought, "I'll use a little collage." He hadn't used this art form since he made the pictures Mrs. Hoffman had hung in her classroom years ago. He ignored rules of illustration and became a child again, working freely as if in a dream. Day after day, he cut shapes from colored paper and pasted them down. He visited his art supply store for some special gray pastel paper for the opening scene, when Peter wakes up in bed to see the snow. Before he could ask, the clerk came over with a roll of Belgian canvas they had just received, excited that Jack could use it for some fine art. Jack bought a narrow strip, leaving the clerk wondering what use he could get from that small piece of canvas. The texture served perfectly for Peter's bed.

In the beginning, Jack thought he would use a bit of patterned paper here and there in the book, but one thing began to lead to another. He bought other patterned paper from Sweden, Italy, Japan, and America. Jack took large sheets of paper and spread white and pastel paints on them with a roller. He cut out hills, and snow piled up in the city. He cut out rectangles of brown, orange, and red and pasted them down, and they transformed into buildings. He cut the mother's dress from oilcloth, which was often used to line cupboards. He spattered India ink on a gray background with a toothbrush for Peter's bedroom wall and carved snowflake patterns from gum erasers and dipped them in pastel colors and stamped them on paper. Snowfall! Feeling like a child playing, he discovered that a piece of red paper with a brown oval could become a boy who walked crunch, crunch, crunch through the snow. His finished work startled him because his way of making art had been transformed. His little friend Peter experienced the snow. When he showed samples to his friends, it was so unlike anything they had seen him do that they asked who had created the pictures. There was pride in his concise answer, "Me."

He sent the first few pages of the book to his editor at Viking Press, Annis Duff, with color pages alternating with black-and-white ones as was often done to cut down on the expense of printing. Ms. Duff insisted they must all be done in full color. Knowing that was expensive, Jack was grateful to her for wanting the book to be at its best. Finally, the book was finished and published. The dedication read, "To Tick, John, and Rosalie."

Jack was forty-six-years old, waking up from what he compared to a twenty-year sleep as he had done commonplace art for a wide range of magazines. He had been in a long nap since he'd used collage in the sweet potato–colored picture he'd brought to Mrs. Hoffman. He wondered if his art still hung in her room. In *The Snowy Day*, he felt as though he had wakened to find himself. Yet, neither he nor his editor could have imagined where the wakeup call of this book would lead.

About the time *The Snowy Day* was published, Jack had done an illustration for a Herbert Gold story in *Playboy*. The magazine sent him a check for more than his bill so he called Chicago and explained the discrepancy to the art director's secretary. She knew nothing about it but promised to get back to him later in the day.

That afternoon, his phone rang, and a voice said, "Long distance, from Chicago."

Not the secretary, but a different voice came through, "Mr. Keats?"

"Yes."

"This is Ruth Gagliardo. Are you sitting down?"

"Huh?"

"I have wonderful news for you. Your book, *The Snowy Day*, has won the Caldecott Award."

Jack thanked her. He had never heard of the Caldecott Award, but she seemed thrilled so he concluded this must be important. He would finish the conversation with her and ask around later to find out what he had won. She swore Jack to secrecy about the award until the press release came out, and as she wound up the call, she asked, "Would you like to make a statement?"

He thought fast. "Well, I'm certainly happy for the little boy in the book."

"Oh, my. How touching. I'll always remember what you said. Your *Snowy Day*, we all believe will be a landmark in children's books." Ruth Gagliardo did, indeed, remember his statement and told the story often. She was also right about the book becoming a landmark.

Soon after he hung up from this first Chicago call, he got a second call, this time from the *Playboy* secretary. There had been no mistake in his check. Her boss liked his drawing and felt it was worth more than Jack had billed.

In order to keep his promise of secrecy to Mrs. Gagliardo, Jack surreptitiously questioned his friends, "What's the Caldecott Award?" and became euphoric at the answers they gave. "It's the greatest award in America you could receive," and "It's awarded to the best book in the country by the American Library Association. If you win it, everyone in the country will know your name."

But one paragraph in his letter from Mrs. Gagliardo confirming his award tempered Jack's elation: "The annual conference of the American Library Association will be held in Chicago this summer. There, on Monday, July 15, the Newbery-Caldecott dinner will be held at the Conrad-Hilton at 7:30 p. m. when you will be presented the medal and will make a ten-minute acceptance address. The dinner will be formal; other details will be sent to you later." The fear it struck remained unmitigated by her closing paragraph: "I shall not forget your gladness 'for the little boy in the book' who is making friends wherever your book goes."

Jack would have to give an acceptance speech in front of 1,800 teachers and librarians. He sometimes became nervous with half a dozen friends just telling a story and making them laugh. But in front of a crowd of strangers? He remembered his high school graduation and couldn't wish for someone to get sick again. He pled with the editor to make his speech, but she assured him that was never done. "You must make it yourself. They've selected your book. Don't worry. They'll all love you, no matter what happens."

No matter what happens. What could happen? Would he faint? Cry in front of all those people? No, he just couldn't make the speech. While he wrung his hands in dread, the publisher dropped into the editor's office. After the editor explained the problem, the publisher sympathized. "I sure know how you feel, Ezra. I had to address a large gathering at a woman's club. As I stood on the podium before the mike, I became aware of a strange thudding sound in the room. I waited for it to subside before I began to speak, when I discovered it was my knees knocking against the podium."

Getting no help from his editor or publisher, Jack visited his therapist and suggested that he might enroll in a Dale Carnegie course in public speaking. The therapist was stern. "Man, you want more pointers and crutches again. No dice. You've got what it takes, and you'll do it."

Jack confided about the award and the speech to Brinton Turkle, his Quaker friend who lived in an old-fashioned boardinghouse and often invited him to dinner. They ate at tables of about six people, and Jack asked his dinner companions if he could practice his speech with them after they ate. They sat quietly, listened to his eight-minute speech, and gave him polite applause. A couple of weeks later, he came back and practiced again.

As time neared for the award, his friend Arthur sent a telegram and a package with a T-shirt and briefs that had a hand-painted Caldecott design. In telegram style it said, "Don't forget to wear your Caldecott underwear good luck."

Finally, the night arrived, and Jack found himself wandering around Chicago in a fearful daze. A friendly young editor, sensitive to his problem, offered to talk to him and help him across the streets. Inside, Jack found his seat on the dais and looked out over the sea of people and heard the buzz of conversation and ripples of laughter. He hardly touched his food. Suddenly the lights dimmed, and a bright spotlight shone on the back doorway. Two waiters, entering with twirling poles with copies of the Caldecott and Newbery Medals, wove through the applauding crowd. Jack popped half a Valium in his mouth to help him relax and made up his mind to read his speech fast and get it over with.

After his introduction, Jack stood to speak. As he heard the familiar sound of his own voice, he slowed down and spoke normally. He finished his speech to great applause and sat down, relieved that he had neither fainted nor cried. Proud of himself, he called his therapist during an intermission to report that he had made the speech without a hitch.

After the banquet, a photographer took an official picture of the award winners. Jack exuded pride with his arms folded across his white dinner jacket. He was shorter than Madeleine L'Engle, who won the Newbery Award for *A Wrinkle in Time*.

Receiving Newbery honor awards in 1963 were Scorche Nic Leodhas for *Thistle and Thyme: Tales and Legends from Scotland* and Olivia Coolidge for *Men of Athens*. Illustrators receiving honor awards were Natalie Maree Belting for *The Sun Is a Golden Earring*, written by Bernada Bryson, and Maurice Sendak for *Mr. Rabbit and the Lovely Present*, written by Charlotte Zolotow.

In his pride for the little boy who became Peter, Jack began to wonder about how long he had saved the strip of pictures. He had moved a number of times and thrown many things away. There had been three years in the Army, a year in Paris, the time with Mira, and the dark discouraging days, but the boy had stayed with him through it all. He checked with *Life* magazine and found the date—13 May 1940. Twenty years had gone by between the time he clipped the pictures and the day he began putting the boy in a picture book. Now twenty-three years later, on 16 July 1963, he had accepted a prestigious award on behalf of the little boy and himself.

On his next scheduled appointment with his therapist, he described the awards banquet and his speech. When he mentioned taking the Valium, the therapist shouted at him. "Schmuck! You had to screw things up, didn't you? You could have done it without turning to some drug for help. The Valium didn't even get a chance to work before your own speech was over."

Jack was amazed. So the pill didn't have time to work? That meant he'd made the speech on his own. So why wasn't the therapist congratulating him on his accomplishment? Jack often felt the therapist gave him too little credit for his achievements and stormed out of a session, but he also saw that the therapist was generous with his time and pushed Jack to do his best work. After a few more years, Jack decided the sessions were counterproductive and gave them up.

Ruth Gagliardo declared in her letter of congratulations for his Caldecott speech that Jack had been simply grand, with no one more pleased than the chairman of the committee, who had the wisdom to choose his book, adding that she thought he looked handsome and anticipated future events they would share.

Apparently, along with giving up the drugs, he also gave up his terror of public speaking or maybe his fear was overwhelmed by the joy he experienced of being heard. Whatever the cause, his life's journey took a U-turn after *The Snowy Day* made his mark in the children's book world.

CHAPTER 10

REACTIONS TO THE SNOWY DAY

ACCOLADES FROM THE PRESS AND FROM INDIVIDUALS FOLlowed the Caldecott Award with emphasis on the significance of the Black child protagonist. In addition to noting that Peter is Black in the announcement that Keats would speak at the Library Council, the *Brooklyn World Telegram* pointed out that native son Keats was a self-taught artist who had attended public schools #149 and #182. Several newspapers, noting that no particular point was made of Peter being a Black child either in the story or the book blurb, suggested that this left an implied feeling of a simple natural occurrence. A different reviewer remarked that this normal incident of a day playing in the snow made it a book for all children.

Keats particularly appreciated supportive letters from leading figures in the African American arts and literary community. Langston Hughes wrote, "THE SNOWY DAY by Ezra Jack Keats is a perfectly charming book. I wish I had some grandchildren to give it to. Yes, I do!"

In a flowery script, Mrs. James Weldon Johnson thanked Keats for his contribution to the Yale Library, where she had contributed her husband's papers, before commenting on *The Snowy Day*:

> It is and time beyond, that I say to you, thank you indeed, for the generous grace of sending to the Memorial Collection of the Yale Library, an inscribed, beautiful picture story that is your very own.
>
> To bring this natural little boy out of an impasse of concept, just fits the time. We who know its significance say, Thank you . . .
>
> James Weldon Johnson would have loved *The Snowy Day*.

Charlemae Rollins, the first Black children's librarian at the Chicago Public Library, to whom Keats would later dedicate *John Henry*, discussed the importance of *The Snowy Day* in an article called, "Progress in Children's Books about the Negro," in the December 1963 issue of *Illinois Libraries*:

> Children's books dealing with the life of the Negro in the United States have made great strides, just as children's books in general have improved in content, illustrations, and format.
>
> As an example, the most coveted award in the field of children's book illustration went to Ezra Jack Keats for his picture book, *The Snowy Day* (Viking, 1962). This delightful picture story of a small boy's first experience alone in the snow was the winner of the Caldecott Medal for 1962. Reviewing the book in the May, 1963 issue of *Elementary English*, Shelton L. Root, Jr., writes, "The Caldecott Medal has gone for a book which, in its own right, richly deserves the distinction. But it marks another event which must be noted. Peter happens to be a Negro. A happier coincidence could hardly have occurred in the children's book field."
>
> Heretofore the area of illustrating has been one of the most sensitive areas in books for children about Negroes. The sharpest criticism has come from readers who objected to many of

the early children's books which presented a stereotyped picture of the Negro child. Happily, this is no longer true—a real cause for celebration.

An elementary school teacher wrote that the art in her classroom changed after she shared *The Snowy Day*. Even though the majority of the children in her classroom were African American, they had regularly used pink paint in self-portraits. After reading the story and seeing the illustrations, they began to use brown paint to depict themselves.

Even better to Keats than the adults who praised the book was that children sent letters and drawings, many of them in their own collage. He was thrilled that they had seen his squares of colored paper as buildings, white bond paper as snow piled up by the gate, or a tan rectangle as a carton.

But not all responses were positive. One man, whose wife had bought *The Snowy Day* at a church bookfair, returned the book to a bookstore looking for the other edition with a white child. The salesman took some effort to convince him there was no white edition.

Keats's joyride hit a pothole in the *Saturday Review* of 11 September 1965, with Dr. Nancy Larrick's article "The All-White World of Children's Books." Her well-taken point that too few protagonists of diverse cultures show up in children's books included a couple of references to Keats's books:

Over the three year period [1962–1964], only four-fifths of one per cent of the children's trade books from the sixty-three publishers tell a story about American Negroes today. Twelve of these forty-four books are the simplest picture books, showing Negroes in the illustrations but omitting the word from the text. Examples are *Benjie* by Joan M. Lexau (Dial Press); *Tony's Birds* by Millicent

Selsam (Harper & Row); *The Snowy Day* and *Whistle for Willie* by Ezra Jack Keats (Viking).

The Caldecott Award went to *The Snowy Day*, written and illustrated by Ezra Jack Keats and published by Viking. The book gives a sympathetic picture of just one child—a small Negro boy. The Negro mother, however is a huge figure in a gaudy yellow plaid dress, albeit without a red bandanna.

Keats did not take the unexpected affront lightly. He fired back a lengthy letter to the editor, published on 2 October:

I was sickened by a reference to me in Nancy Larrick's article. She refers to an illustration of mine from *The Snowy Day* saying "The Negro mother, however, is a huge figure in a gaudy yellow plaid dress, albeit without a red bandanna." The dress is gaily colored as is everything else in the book. What is wrong with a mother being "huge"? What if she were white?

I wish Miss Larrick would not project upon me the stereotypes in her own mind—or in others. If she sees a figure of a large Negro mother and associates it with a red bandana, that is her problem, not mine. The Caldecott Committee, which awarded the medal to *The Snowy Day*, had three Negro members whose total commitment, sensitivity, and understanding is well known; [they] did not have this reaction. For years now, I have been receiving letters from teachers, children, and parents, both Negro and white, in praise of the book.

I, too, wrote an article for the *Saturday Review* of November 9, 1963, which concluded with, "If any group of people is to be pictured as always fashionably thin, with children who never misbehave, and all of them improbably perfect, we are denying a people's right to deal with reality and assume the very responsibilities for which they struggle. All people want is the opportunity to be people.

"Let us open the book covers, these long-shut doors, to new and wonderful, true and inspiring books for all children about all children—the tall and short, fat and thin, dark and light, beautiful and homely. Welcome!"

Now, as for her other objection that Negroes are portrayed in picture books but are not mentioned as Negroes. In a book for children three to six years of age, where the color of one's skin makes it clear who is Negro and who is white, is it arbitrarily necessary to append racial tags? Might I suggest armbands?

I dread to think of what the children's book field would be like if we follow such a Savonarola-like way of thinking.

A final, more cheerful note—this morning I passed a neighbor who called, "I just saw a reproduction from *The Snowy Day* in the *Saturday Review*. It looked just beautiful!"

According to his friend Martin Pope, if Keats had a stereotype at all in his mind, it was that of a typical mother. Most mothers with whom he was acquainted, including his own, had lost any sylphlike shape to the starchy diet they could afford. Their good homemade bread and potato soup did not lend itself to slim figures. Confirmation of this conclusion seems to come in Keats's portrayal of a white mother of the same proportions and color-ful attire in *Louie's Search* and *Regards to the Man in the Moon*.

Librarians and parents rallied to Keats's defense with letters to the editor, as illustrated by the following excerpted examples:

I deplore and protest the total misconception and misrepresenta-tion Nancy Larrick gave to an illustration she singled out from Ezra Jack Keats's, "*The Snowy Day*," and cruelly dissected in her article, "The All-White World of Children's Books."

Rarely was there ever a picture book more warmly received in The World of Children's Books—this and its sequel, "Whistle for Willie," were created with charming simplicity and will live forever in the hearts of children; only an artist who knows and loves children of all races and creeds could express his "gift" in such distinctive picture books. That Ezra Jack Keats won the 1963 Caldecott Award for "*The Snowy Day*" was a joyful announcement; his dedication and determination to give only his <u>very best</u> to children "paid off"!

Librarian Irene Roop in Connecticut

Miss Larrick's criticism of books in which Negroes appear in the illustrations but the word is omitted from the text is striking evidence of a worthy cause obscuring a writer's perspective. No Negro, especially a child, has "being a Negro" on his mind at all times. Sometimes "being a person" takes precedence.

Ezra Jack Keats' book *The Snowy Day*, for example, presents the experiences of a human child responding to a natural phenomenon. Most children, Negro and white, have responded to snow and could relate personal [*sic*] to the story. Further, Negroes in the illustrations preclude the possibility of any false barrier between a young Negro reader and the experience. What more could be done? The word "Negro" in this text would be irrelevant and inappropriate.

Charlene Slivnick, Washington. D. C.

In rebuttal to Miss Larrick's article, "TAWWOCB," SR, September 11, 1965: while Miss Larrick's point of view that more books containing Negro children should be published is a fine one, why all the quibbling when something very good is finally written. Mr. Ezra Keats' Caldecott Award winning book A SNOWY DAY, is a fine and sensitive effort. To attack one of the illustrations because it happens to be a large and colorfully dressed Negro mother is as foolish as demanding that we change the name of The White House and the Blackbird. This kind of picky-une criticism is sheer willful negation of a superb work.

> Carole F. Schwartz, Former Faculty Member of Hunter Graduate School and The New School of Social Research

Keats, not willing to let the subject die, referenced the article in a letter to the *Education Review* with a very purposeful postscript:

> P. S. I just remembered having finished a book about four months ago which had a "huge" white woman, and a collection of very fashionable looking women, both white and Negro. "Now what does all this waist-measuring and skin-tagging really add up to?
> Not a thing!"

Larrick responded again in the 17 September *Saturday Review*:

> Dear Mr. Keats:
> I certainly did not mean to suggest that an author should necessarily use the term "Negro" in the text of a story about a Negro child.
> Consequently, I am not in sympathy with your proposal that armbands be used. I like your Willie the way he is!

Intent on setting the record exactly straight, Keats made his final response on 20 September:

> I have just received a response to my letter from Nancy Larrick. She says she did not mean to say that an author should necessarily use the term Negro in the text of a story. She says, "I like your Willie just the way he is!"

However, in her article (Page 64, column 1) she says, "The Snowy Day" and "Whistle for Willie" are examples of "showing Negroes in the illustration but omitting the word from the text!"

Ellen Tarry puts a balanced perspective on Larrick's efforts to be inclusive while defending Keats's work in a 20 September 1965 letter to the editor of *Saturday Review*. She also touches on issues that endure as the children's book world continues to seek the presence of all children on its pages:

As a Negro and an author of children's books, your controversial article by Nancy Larrick, "The All-White World of Children's Books," which appeared in the issue of September 11, 1965, was of special interest to me.

It is quite true that there was a time when it was most difficult to find books for children by or about Negroes. My own efforts in this connection grew out of experiences with my fifth grade Negro students in Birmingham, Alabama, more than thirty years ago.

However, there have always been a few publishers who have dared to publish books which they felt filled a need—regardless of whether the hero was a Negro or not.

As early as 1942, May Massee, then Editor of Junior Books, Viking Press, Inc., published my *Hezekiah Horton*. By 1946, Viking had also published *Jaspar, the Drummin' Boy*, by Margaret Taylor, and *My Dog Rinty*, to which Miss Larrick referred in her article. In 1950, Viking published *The Runaway Elephant* by this writer. Ezra Jack Keats' *The Snowy Day* and *Whistle for Willie* came out in 1963 and 1964, I believe.

Many good children's books about other ethnic groups were also published by this same firm. One or two other publishing firms did likewise. Though courageous publishers who would risk a possible loss were few, they were not completely lacking.

Publishers must accept some of the blame for catering to the tastes of a biased American reading public. At the same time, those of us who were converted did not always put our dollars where we put our mouths. In other words, the enlightened reading public did not indicate its preferences at the cash registers of book stores. But for sales to schools and libraries, *My Dog Rinty* and *Hezekiah Horton* would have long since been out of print like *The Runaway Elephant*, which made the list of the 100 most beautiful books published in 1950—before Birmingham, Montgomery, or Selma.

Let us hope that the social revolution, of which we are all a part will be reflected in our book purchases. Publishers must still be concerned with profit and loss.

Beside my concern that Miss Larrick's article lumped all publishers on the side unattended by angels, I thought her reference to the plump Negro mother in *The Snowy Day* was snide and unwarranted. I am a stout Negro mother and my daughter has enjoyed a big lap to sit in and ample bosom on which to lean in times of trouble. I saw Ezra Jack Keats' mother to Peter before the book was published and commented on the fact that she was a solid security symbol. I loved her colorful house dress, too.

You and Miss Larrick have also performed an important service inasmuch as you have brought into the open a subject which has been under the table too long.

Putting some of the furor behind them, Larrick continued working for diversity through her teaching and writing, particularly through her advocacy work in the International Reading Association, now the International Literacy Association. In the meantime, bolstered by his and Peter's success, Keats returned home to find new stories to tell.

ℳANY ℬOOKS

BACK IN HIS STUDIO, KEATS CLAIMED THAT PETER AND HIS friends chatted with each other, plotting for more adventures while he eavesdropped. Turning on the lights at night, he would hear the characters talking, but their story would not be what he had been writing. When he brought the manuscript with the revisions to his editor, she might remind him that it did not contain the story they had agreed upon. He explained that the kids in the book had told him what to do. Both the books and the children who populated them came alive to Keats. Soon he was too busy and having too much fun writing the stories of his imaginary friends to illustrate many books or book jackets for other people. Phyllis Whitney was sorry to lose her jacket cover artist.

Reminiscent of his mother's lemonade, Keats took the tartness and flavor of his own life, added sweetener, and created an idealized childhood. Overtly and subtly, he included people who were important to him in his storylines and in his artwork. The stories he wrote sometimes mirrored his memories and sometimes adjusted his own experience to make a more kid-friendly world.

Peter reappears in Keats's next book *Whistle for Willie* (1964) and in a series of picture books that reflect the memories of the ex-kid. Using his brother's name, Willie, for the pet dog Keats had longed for but could never have, Peter learns to whistle for him. Using chalk drawings in an errand to the grocery store, Peter replicates Ezra's way of doing childhood chores. However, unlike his own parents, Keats gives Peter loving and supportive parents who are thrilled with his accomplishment.

Keats's perception of himself as the unwanted new baby shows up in *Peter's Chair* (1967). Peter copes with his unhappiness over this new sibling in the same way a young disgruntled Ezra had dealt with his discontent by running away from home. An idealistic childhood twist comes when Peter's mother pleads for him to return and Peter has a change of heart as he helps paint his outgrown chair in pink for the baby sister.

Peter struggles through a thunderstorm to mail an invitation to his friend Amy (*A Letter to Amy*, 1968) for his upcoming birthday party. The background features the graffiti of city streets with amusing glimpses of Willie checking things out.

Adding Archie to the next Peter books reflects his own close relationship with Itch. Bullies show up in *Goggles* (1969), but they are outsmarted by Peter and Archie, aided and abetted by Willie. Rooftop clotheslines, featured in his art, allude to his early days peering from his window at the colors of clothes waving in the breeze.

Peter becomes the supporting character when a cat plays havoc with Archie's magic trick in *Hi, Cat* (1970), and his friend Archie wins a prize for the quietest pet in the pet show (*Pet Show*, 1972), where one of the judges looks like Keats himself.

When Keats looked at this series of books, he was surprised to see Peter getting older. Keats first noticed the growth when Peter could not fit into his chair. It seemed that, though he painted the pictures, Peter had grown up all by himself.

Peter does not appear in the final book in this series, which features his friends. Central to the idea in *Dreams* (1974) is the puppet shadow that saves Archie's cat from a snarling dog.

Apt. 3 (1971) has the closest resemblance to the tenement where Keats grew up. Sam and Ben make their way through the building's stairways—stairways as dark as those where young Ezra pawned off his fake stamps. The boys look for the source of some unusual music, while hearing and smelling emanations from all the apartments. Sam lingers outside Betsy's door hoping she will make an appearance as Ezra had once made his way past Harriet's house hoping to see her on the porch. The boys are surprised that their blind neighbor uses his other senses to know the other tenement dwellers as well as they do, including knowing about Sam's crush on Betsy.

The pets Ezra could not have in childhood hung out in his studio and populated his books. In his studio, his dog Jake and his cat Samantha supervised his work. In the Peter and Archie books, the dog Willie functions as another character. Other animals appeared in almost wordless books. These books, with fewer newsprint collages, revert to his artistic bent and training and feature animals instead of people as characters.

Keats watched children skating in front of his house, falling, clinging, and performing slapstick-like maneuvers. He remembered a little boy in a large woolen hat pulled down so far he could barely see where he was going. As he passed a nearby corner, he saw a German shepherd sitting with his paws out of the window watching the world go by. Combining these three ideas, he produced *Skates!* (1973) with two dogs having amusing mishaps as they learn to skate. After almost giving up, they rescue a kitten with a big hat. Books like *Skates!*, *Psst! Doggie* (1973), and *Kitten for a Day* (1973) hint at the vestige of a kid's nature that is still part of him. In *Maggie and the Pirate* (1979), Maggie discovers a cricket and puts him in a tiny cage. The pet is similar to the only kind young Ezra could have had, and the adult author sympathizes with Maggie's despair as she looks for her lost cricket.

Louie (1975) introduces a character whose name is the same as his eccentric uncle and his brother's pal who befriended him as a child. Louie has significant similarities to Keats's own early years. In the first of four books that feature Louie as the protagonist, this quiet lonely child is often made fun of by other children. He finds friends who reach out to him with a puppet named Gussie, who becomes a catalyst for new relationships. Like Ezra, Louie fills his loneliness with crayons, drawing pictures in the background similar to those Ezra drew around his mother's table. In an amusing spread in *The Trip* that could be used to prove the point that Keats never became an "ex-kid," snapshots of real children watching out their windows form part of a collage as Louie takes his friends on an imaginary plane trip. The "kid" in the top left corner is the adult Keats.

Louie finds himself unnoticed even as he strolls down the street wearing funny props in *Louie's Search* (1980). In the boy's search for a father, Keats returns for a model to the zaddik who had chased him years ago. Now, with an artistic education behind him, he recreates the red-haired, dust-covered giant he remembered, looking like a bizarre, unkempt, dirty version of Michelangelo's Moses—a perfect model for the junkman Barney in his story, although the face is Keats's own. Barney's pursuit of Louie, rendered in silhouette, captures the one he described when the zaddik chased him, and just like young Ezra, Louie's first encounter with the junkman leaves him "so scared, he couldn't speak." Keats creates an ending even better than his own discovery of the zaddik's gift of a board for painting. He reveals the junkman as a man with a gentle heart, good enough to be a stepfather, and pictures Louie sitting atop the shoulders of a somewhat cleaned-up Barney at the wedding to his mother.

In the fourth Louie book, *Regards to the Man in the Moon* (1981), Keats continues the reclamation of the junkman. In his story set in a multicultural neighborhood, children leave their mockery of Barney behind when they take an imaginary trip to the moon using the junk he has collected. Though the book's view of space is fictional, Keats consulted with his scientist friend Martin Pope for details.

With few exceptions, the backdrop for Keats's books is the beauty he saw in the city, a setting different from most children's books of that era. Graffiti appears almost constantly, the laundry waves regularly between the roofs of the tall tenement buildings, and the city stoplight becomes an icon.

Ideas for Keats's stories, apart from the series books, turned up everywhere. One day, he saw an interesting painting about as big as a postage stamp. The picture showed an older couple, sitting with their palms held out filled with birdseed. Pigeons perched on their shoulders and ate out of their hands. That gave him an idea for a girl character. Jennie turned a plain old hat into a work of art with the help of some birds who brought her collage roses, swans, and a pink valentine. He called the book *Jennie's Hat* (1966).

Five books published between 1965 and 1971 depart from his work with children's fiction, but not from his attention to the commonality of people. Adding one of his favorite techniques of marbleized paper to his use of collage and paint, he retells folklore in *John Henry: an American Legend* (1965).

God Is in the Mountain (1966) has his choice of quotations from a multitude of religions, illustrated in shades of black, orange, and white using cutouts and wash techniques. Its cover blurb claims it is a book for all ages. His foreword addresses his respect for all people:

> This is a collection of voices and intimations.
> They speak to us from different times and different places.
> What they have in common is the awareness of a dimension without which life is indeed meaningless.
> I should like to share these glimpses into the Way offered us—
> beautiful and potent, within us and around us, ever present and
>   waiting. EJK

Using bright colors and his signature collage, Keats illustrated the traditional Christmas song *The Little Drummer Boy* (1968). His portrayal of Mary and the baby for the line "Then He smiled at me" brings to mind his childhood glimpse inside the cathedral to see "a statue of a lady with a shawl over her head holding a baby, tenderly and sadly." Keats's empathy with the drummer boy can be felt in the spread for "I am a poor boy, too."

Night (1969) departs from any of his other work. Done totally in black with photographs by Beverly Hall, it quotes from a wide range of authors: John Milton, Langston Hughes, Dylan Thomas, James Joyce, and others. Selections indicate his gamut of literary interests, with his artistic eye providing background for the photographs on black paper with white lettering.

Taking the traditional children's song, he uses bright and dark colors, collage, marbleized paper, and paint to create *Over in the Meadow* (1971) with humor that will appeal to any young child as they count and repeat the activities of the various animals.

Keats had almost completely abandoned illustrating for other writers by the time he made an exception for Florence Freedman's book *Two Tickets to Freedom* (1971), the true story of Ellen and William Craft, an enslaved couple escaping to freedom, with the light-skinned wife disguised as a southern planter and her darker husband portraying her slave. Turning the story into a picture book was a special task about a subject of great importance to Keats and to his old friend and teacher. The starkness of his black-and-white drawings fit the story and would be the last work he did in this style.

In what would be the final book in his lifetime, *Clementina's Cactus* (Viking, 1982), he revisits memories of a vacation trip to Colorado, Arizona, and New Mexico years earlier with Itch and Lillie and their daughters Miriam and Deborah. This wordless book is filled with scenes that he had seen with them in the desert. A prereader follows the wonder shared by father and daughter as they watch for the bloom arising in the desert. It would be Keats's final ideal image of family in the shared father and daughter experience of astonishment and awe.

Keats described his process as being like a silent movie that he saw acted out with his own words coming through. He put his illustrations on the wall and kept coming back to them to see them choreographed together, aware of scale, color, composition, and movement that allowed him to make judgments in interpreting the story. In his reflections on his process for writing, Keats noticed how the writing and art intertwined.

Keats brought children into his studio to model for poses he needed and sometimes modeled himself and painted his own picture into the books. Keats, like the children, enjoyed seeing himself in the finished books.

New things for his collages came from odd places. A friend might rush into his studio with news of a trashcan outside filled with discarded wallpaper. Keats would hurry out and go through the trash, sheet by sheet, to find several good pieces for new projects.

In what must have been another unexpected development, Keats's books opened doors for him to travel and for speaking engagements for librarians, teachers, and children's book aficionados who wanted to know his process. For Keats, the parades and celebrations were enjoyable, but having his voice heard and respected was even more satisfying.

CHAPTER 12

THE JAPANESE CONNECTION

AS CHILDREN IN THE UNITED STATES WATCHED FOR KEATS'S next picture book, *The Snowy Day* was translated into sixteen languages. Keats was particularly amused at the different sounds Peter made walking through the snow in his international travels. His feet sounded, "crunch, crunch, crunch" in the United States and England; "nar, nar, nar" in Sweden; "krunj, krunj, krunj" in Norway; "narshun, narshun, narshun" in Finland; and "krick, krick, krick" in Denmark. In Japan, the sound was very tiny: "kyu, kyu, kyu."

Japan became one of Jack's favorite destinations. His first Japanese visit came when Franklin Watts decided to publish three of his books in Japanese and sent him there to deliberate with the book printers. Since he remembered loving Japanese art during his high school days, Keats anticipated the trip with great delight. He was not prepared for his reception.

Twelve librarians met him at the airport, one of them bringing a huge bouquet of flowers. They asked where he wanted to go and what sights he wanted to visit. Keats gave them a list of things he had planned to see and do, thinking they'd give him directions and help him plan his tour. Instead, they saw themselves as his personal tour guides and escorted him to all the places on his list. His interpreter, Sachiko Saionji, helped him work with artists, writers, and publishers. In addition to making friends with the book publishers, he became acquainted with some Japanese children and their mothers.

Keats joined a caravan with the Bamboo Shoot Library under the direction of the Hakuko Foundation that traveled around Tokyo to settlement houses, day care centers, parks, and schools and watched their staff read to children. Following World War II, the Japanese people were determined that their children would have books presented with the sense of drama one would find in the theater. Bamboo Shoot staff demonstrations trained mothers, librarians, and teachers with techniques that involved children in the literature. Keats listened to readers dramatize the books using small voices for small sounds that became louder as the sounds increased. He listened to the leaders telling ghost stories that chilled the blood and cooled off the children even in hot weather. He delighted in their puppet shows, loving the sense of theater in all their performances with books.

The only problem from the trip arose when he returned home and had to find space in his Manhattan apartment for the many gifts his new Japanese friends had bestowed on him, often handmade or personal tributes. He shared his many new trip stories with his friends, ending with, "It was one of the most exhilarating and lovely experiences in my life, and I can't wait to go back." He would return to Japan several times for different reasons.

One return trip came because of the spunky dogs in his book *Skates!* Miss Saionji wrote him a letter telling him what happened after he left Japan. A home library mother loved the book so much that she bought a pair of skates for her son. The little boy skated and was soon joined by neighborhood children who skated with him in spite of warnings by the schools that skating could cause a dangerous car accident in Tokyo traffic.

The children decided to ask for a public skating rink. When their mothers agreed, all of them marched down to the mayor's office to plead for a safe place to skate. The mayor was not interested. Not ready to give up, the mothers continued to visit the mayor day after day. Finally, one of the mothers brought a drawing of a skating dog Keats had done with a black felt tip pen for her on the last day of his visit. The mayor smiled, said he liked the little picture, and added that the children could have a skating rink to be finished by the end of the year.

Miss Saionji ended her letter, "Hooray! For the children, for the mother, and for you. We are dreaming of another conclusion, though, that the very person who caused all this to happen come back as an honored guest for the opening of the rink." In her continued correspondence to explain building delays, she said that *The Snowy Day* had gone into its second edition with a correction of "a black artist" to "an international artist"—a mistake not confined to the Japanese since many people, even American librarians, assumed that only a Black artist would have put a Black child in a book.

Miss Saionji's wish was granted, and Keats returned as the guest of honor at the opening of the skating rink. He joined the mayor to cut the ribbon, releasing clusters of balloons into the air. Exhibition skaters entertained the kids before Keats made a short speech and signed a plaque. The new skating rink was named for him.

With the gracious hospitality and pleasure Keats experienced on this trip, it came as a surprise to him that they paid him for addressing conferences of artists and writers—in money they had gift wrapped so he could not refuse it. He responded by donating the money to the Riverdale and Spuyten Duyvil Branches of the

New York Public Library in the neighborhood where the most
Japanese immigrants lived so they could buy books in Japanese
for children who had not yet learned English.

An unexpected event brought yet another trip to Japan. In
June 1977 while Keats was preparing for major prostate surgery,
he received a different kind of letter. A Japanese mother wrote
about her nine-year-old son's death after being hit by a car. Akira
had been four years old when Keats visited Japan and signed
Peter's Chair, which she said had become his dearest treasure. She
told how he loved for her to read the autograph "for Akira Ishida."

The mother continued the letter by saying she had recently
checked *Dreams* out of the library. It was the last book Akira read
before his death. Her letter ended:

> I picture to myself what kind of dream he is dreaming now in
> heaven. I believe he was happy to have read *Dreams* as his last
> book. The last time I saw him, I put his treasure *Peter's Chair* into
> his coffin. I hope you will be kind enough to pray for the soul of
> Akira and also hope you will write more beautiful and dreamy
> illustrated books for him, too. I enclose his picture.
>
>   Yours sincerely,
>   Toshiko Ishida

Keats showed the letter to Mrs. Hall, his weekly cleaning
woman, and they cried over it together. "It's a terrible tragedy.
But I'm also crying because there's some beautiful soulful music
in it," she said.

Keats planned a visit to see the Ishida family and called his
surgeon to postpone his surgery. The doctor protested that he
was taking a big risk of having blockage that would become an
emergency and necessitate being flown back to the United States.

A stubborn Keats decided to take his chances and booked the next available flight to Japan.

The Ishigamis, his friends in Tokyo, were moved by Akira's story. They offered to meet Jack, travel on the train with him, and serve as translators. They rode the train for an hour and a half to Hasuda City. Observing the landscape much like he had done years before as he traveled the El with his father, he noticed signs done in calligraphy in all shapes, sizes, and colors; laundry and clothing hung out from open windows; ancient Japanese architecture; new homes, buildings, and factory smokestacks; and smaller towns and housing complexes. The landscape seemed to be an endless collage from Tokyo to Hasuda City. Mr. Ishigami explained that Hasuda City was a "bed town," a place with more comfort than crowded Tokyo with a few undeveloped areas, empty lots, and trees, but not a rural area.

Mrs. Ishida met the train and took them first to the cemetery. The black marble family tombstone had only one name: Akira. Keats followed their instructions in the Buddhist tradition, maybe remembering how important traditions were in his own home and community. He dipped a wooden ladle into a wooden bucket and poured the water over the tombstone. He placed lilies he'd brought at the base of the stone and said a silent prayer for Akira before lingering at a respectful distance while the mother stood before the tomb.

Mr. Ishida, a patent attorney for the Japanese printer who produced the Keats books and the reason Akira had met Keats on the first trip, greeted them at their small modest home and provided slippers as they took off their shoes. They were treated to a lunch prepared by Yuko, Akira's twelve-year-old sister.

After lunch, Mrs. Ishida told Akira's story. He had been happy when the family moved from Tokyo to Hasuda City because he loved insects and could follow his interests. His friends uncovered a stone, found a group of bugs, and began to stomp on them, but Akira stopped them. He was fascinated by this world of largely unseen creatures that most people did not notice. On the sixth of June in the late afternoon, he set out with his butterfly net after preparing jars at home for feeding his catch before he released them again. He chased a butterfly down the road past a useless high brick wall when a car came from the other side. Neither the driver nor Akira could see each other. Akira was killed instantly.

Mrs. Ishida took Keats into another room with a small shrine crowned with Akira's photograph and filled with the sweet smell of incense. As Keats knelt to pray, he noticed his books that they had read together at the foot of the shrine. His visit ended with talk around the kitchen table and listening to a recording of Akira playing the upright piano and singing happy birthday to Akira's father in Japanese and English.

The next day Keats gave a speech at a Tokyo university. Someone had told his interpreter, Mrs. Yogo, about the reason for his return to Japan and about his illness. She explained that her husband was a doctor and asked him to write down the name of his problem, and within half an hour of dropping him off at his hotel, her husband and four children arrived. The doctor assured him that every department of the Tokyo hospital had been alerted that he should receive the best of attention if he became ill. Keats did not need to use the doctors, but his spirits were lifted by the four children who wanted to sit on his lap and hold his hand.

Keats made one more trip out to see the Ishidas before he returned home to have his surgery. After he returned to the United States, he and Mrs. Ishida continued to write to each other for as long as he lived. When Jack's book *The Trip* was published, the Japanese version was dedicated to Akira.

$\mathcal{M}$ANY $\mathcal{L}$ETTERS, $\mathcal{M}$ANY $\mathcal{R}$OADS

AFTER HIS BOOKS BECAME POPULAR, KEATS'S MAILBOX STAYED full with a variety of correspondence. He received requests for assistance with an array of projects to benefit children. Admirers trying to assist with his collages sent clippings from old books, patterns, and pieces of paper. Children sent little books showing their efforts to use his technique. Accumulation of an abundance of letters from children and teachers and a delay in sending them to Keats occasionally caused some testiness. Keats protested in a 3 June 1969 letter to Velma Varner at Viking: "These letters had been sent to me by children, teachers and librarians, some needing immediate answers in connection with their work. Apparently, whoever handles this must have let the letters accumulate since January. I think such a practice is appalling . . ."

In a turnaround letter, Ms. Varner agreed that the delay was appalling and promised that it would not happen again.

Keats particularly loved the stacks of letters he received from children and answered them promptly, putting their enclosed school pictures or snapshots on his studio walls. He took pride that the photographs of children with many skin colors came from around the world and claimed the only thing he minded about answering his mail was getting writer's cramp.

Keats answered a request from the Essex County School Library Association for the donation of an original illustration to give as a door prize at an author tea with two stipulations: (1) that it must be given to a school or library where it would stay permanently, and (2) that he would be informed of the ultimate recipient and the location of the picture. The last piece in this correspondence from Miss Doris Feczko, dated 11 December 1968, expressed gratitude and gave the name of the librarian and the library where it would be placed in "the race troubled city of Newark. It is exactly what I hoped for and I'm sure you did, too."

One letter came from Louise Proffitt. As a proofreader for her newspaper in Moorhead City, North Carolina, she noticed an article about a children's author named Ezra Jack Keats. She had purchased a painting done by an artist with that name in 1952, when she was Mrs. Paul Cleland. The local elementary school librarian told her this children's author had once done murals in his early career. Her letter said, "I am wondering, although you are now a well-known author of children's books, if you are the artist whose painting I have. . . . I would appreciate it very much if you would use the enclosed, self-addressed envelope to let me know if you can recollect having done this painting."

Keats answered her letter by telling her the name of the hotel where she and her husband had stayed and the name of the shoe store where she had bought the painting. In her reply, Mrs. Proffitt explained that she had been unaware of Keats's work because she had no children. She invited him to come see the painting that had given her so much pleasure if he was ever in the area.

Keats wrote letters to his niece Bonnie from his dog Jake. Jake supposedly signed them and drew his self-portrait. Bonnie answered with letters to Jake and cautioned him about confidential things he should not tell "Uncle Jack."

One day his mail contained an invitation from his old friend Florence Freedman, now a professor at Hunter College. She asked Keats to join other children's authors for "Tea and Talk" sessions with her students. Mrs. Freedman remembered Mrs. Katz's concern for others she had seen years ago in her kitchen and saw it again in the children Keats put into his books.

Business mail came as well. With a keen eye to how he wanted his work used, one exchange with a Swedish publisher included a strong preference that *A Letter to Amy* not be changed to their more common name Anna. Another request for permission to use parallel Black and North Carolina Piedmont white dialects for *Whistle for Willie* forwarded to him from Viking prompted an even firmer denial from Keats. He sent a strong request for a copy of Viking's refusal letter to be certain it had been sent. Other letters to and from editors contained protests and apologies as Keats stood up for his books and their portrayal and placement in publishing catalogs, and there were detailed discussions with Weston Woods for filmstrips of his books. Some letters planned arrangements for school visits and donations and were followed up with thank you notes back and forth with the participants.

He received an invitation to *Who's Who in America* in 1976 and to *Who's Who in Black America* in 1975. That common mistake, seen also with his Japanese friends, assumed once again that only someone who was Black himself would have made a Black child the protagonist in a children's book.

Editor Ursula Nordstrom, hinting at Keats's practice of moving from publisher to publisher, wrote a letter about *Peter's Chair* that began, "I suppose you are out helling around with another children's book editor—and I hate her."

Assorted mail might include a one-time request to use *Goggles* for no fee on Children's Network Television, an expiration notice for a driver's license restricted to corrective lenses, or a response from Jim Henson to assure Keats that he is worrying needlessly about the departure of Kermit, who is near and dear to the hearts of Henson Associates.

A letter might come from his traveling friend Martin Pope about the Popes' full schedule saying his lectures were going well, recounting being honored for his sixtieth birthday in Peking, and adding information about the promotion that he and Lillie continued for Ezra's work: "Your books and posters are a smash hit. We whip them out at appropriate points in our visits and our hosts are delighted. They have been given to a Children's Palace and two kindergartens. Today, the regular schools open after vacation and since Lillie visits schools while I teach, she will be taking them to the regular school classes."

As much as Keats enjoyed his mail, this was only the beginning of the pleasure that would come to him from his books. The child Ezra, with his longing to be heard, grown into the man Keats finally found satisfaction as recognition and appreciation came from the world of child advocacy. The popularity of his books gave him credibility, recognition, and the voice that young Ezra had sought at the supper table. The children's book world, and by extension the children's literacy world, perceived him as someone who loved and understood children and cared about their development. Those who shared his concerns began to call for his art and his expertise with one commitment often leading to the next.

The US Information Agency requested a loan of the original illustration of Peter reminiscing in the bathtub about his snow adventures from *The Snowy Day* to include in its overseas exhibit *Graphic Arts USA*. They documented showings from 5 October 1963 through 24 October 1965 in the USSR, listing showings in Rumania, Czechoslovakia, Poland, and Yugoslavia with a total attendance of 2,998,898, and asked for an extension of the loan from 1 March 1966 for at least another year. The ending would not be quite so joyful. In a 10 October 1967 letter to Viking Press, Robert S. Byrnes, acting chief of the Exhibits Division apologized profusely for the loss of his painting. He said the illustration was widely acclaimed and cast great credit on the United States, but they were shocked to find it missing along with several other items when the exhibit was returned. After an exhaustive search, they had reached the conclusion that recovery was not possible and were sending an insurance check for the value of five hundred dollars that Keats had placed on the painting. As a small consolation, Mr. Byrnes added that procedures were now in place to prevent such an unfortunate occurrence in the future.

With an international reputation as a children's book writer and illustrator, Keats became a logical choice to design promotional work for United Nations International Children's Emergency Fund (UNICEF). From 1965 to 1982, he designed their posters and cards and served as judge for a children's art contest. He took great satisfaction from a letter he received from them reporting the sale of three million cards in the United States with two hundred thousand dollars in proceeds. He reveled in the idea that the money would treat 200,000 tuberculosis patients or provide enough medicine to protect 2,800,000 children from malaria for a year. Success of the UNICEF cards led to a request from the American Artist Group for him to submit designs for their Christmas card line.

Lloyd N. Morrisett, vice-president of Carnegie Corporation, wondered if television could become a more effective educator and threw out the idea at a 1966 dinner party. This prompted Joan Ganz Cooney to do a study called "The Potential Uses of Television in Preschool Education," which led to a proposal she submitted to Carnegie in February 1968. She had produced a number of documentaries for noncommercial television, including a Harlem precursor to Head Start, but she had concluded that a different approach aimed directly at children would make a more effective learning tool. Ultimately, this proposal would lead to the Children's Television Network. While she hoped it would help all children, she believed it would be a failure if the needs of disadvantaged children were not met. Her goal was to have a multicultural cast including both sexes with no star in a program that supplemented but did not replace classroom activity, a perfect fit for Keats's own agenda and work. In the summer seminar that would begin the process on 8–10 July 1968, the stated goal was "defining curricular goals for language and reading that would be priorities for subsequent television production." Keats was the only children's author selected to join. The show called *Sesame Street* launched in November 1969 on almost two hundred public and commercial stations.

In similar fashion, Lynda Johnson Robb began a correspondence with Keats in 1968. She asked if she could send her recently purchased copy of *The Snowy Day* for an autograph and followed by telling him in her thank you note that she had shared the book with Mrs. Robert McNamara for inclusion in her Reading Is Fundamental program. The national program distributed free books to children, and Lynda Robb helped start a group in her Northern Virginia community. Keats's friendly correspondence with her would continue off and on during his lifetime, covering such diverse topics as a suggestion from Keats, after she mentioned difficulties with finding bilingual literary choices, that she might consider his enclosed *My Dog Is Lost* in her list, congratulatory notes on her husband's elections, and thank you notes from her for signing books for her own children.

In a news release in late 1969, Harvard University announced a gift to the Harvard Graduate School of Education Library. The gift included sketches, drafts, original art work for Mr. Keats's books, and a collection of correspondence from children and national figures. Noted in the release were Keats's use of collage and his acclaim for the portrayal of Black children, as well as a sample list of his children's books. Correspondence between Harvard and Keats about archiving his work continued through 1976, with the materials ultimately returned to Keats, who housed them in Manhattan.

Not shy about speaking up in letters to editors about anything he saw as injustice, Keats took offense in one notable exchange at the criticism of Maurice Sendak's *Where the Wild Things Are* by Dr. Bruno Bettelheim in an article for the March 1969 *Ladies Home Journal* titled "The Care and Feeding of Monsters." Without reading Sendak's book and with nothing more than expressed concerns from three mothers about giving a child a book about monsters, Dr. Bettelheim castigated the book, claiming that the basic anxiety of the child is desertion. He went on to label being sent to bed alone as one desertion and without food as a second desertion, with the combination representing the worst desertion that could threaten a child. Keats rose to the book's defense.

In his letter, Keats shares his astonishment that Dr. Bettelheim would enter into an elaborate analysis of the book on the basis of hearsay rather than reserving judgment until he had read it. He makes several points in his lengthy letter:

> The book, contrary to one of Dr. Bettelheim's arbitrary assumptions, was written for enjoyment, not as therapy for disturbed children. Written and illustrated by a master at the art of communicating with children, it comes off as a subtle, tongue-in-cheek romp.... Nowhere in the article does Dr. Bettelheim explore the possibility that the source of the child's fear may spring from the home situation rather than from the book itself.... I do believe Dr. Bettelheim wound up being controlled by the parents in his discussion group.

In his response letter to the editor, Dr. Bettelheim admits that he had not read the book at the time of the discussion but claims that he read it before the column went to press and confirmed his original conclusion.

Beginning in October 1970, Keats was often a guest on the popular children's television show *Mister Rogers' Neighborhood*. In an episode that aired on 1 April 1971, he drops by with a press sheet of one of his books. Chatting with Fred Rogers like an old friend and foreshadowing a relationship that was to come, he explains the process of making books and shares two paintings, one of his parents and another of the rooftop of the building where he lived as a boy. In the episode for 9 May 1972, Keats visits Someplace Else in the Neighborhood of Make-Believe, participating in some confusing events before reading the story of a bad king named Donkey Hodie. The 22 February 1974 show opens with a post card from Keats showing Mt. Fuji that said he had returned from Japan and would be visiting that day. When he arrives, he shows pictures and mementos from his trip and shares his book *Skates!*, noting that it prompted a town in Japan to build a skating rink.

Perhaps the episode that best captures the spirit of both men is Keats demonstrating the making of marbleized paper as the two "ex-kids" share amazement at the way the oils mingle on the paper to produce unexpected designs and shades of color. That childlike wonder, still alive in both men, and their love for children formed a bond that would last the rest of their lives.

In 1972, Syd Hoff, who had made a reputation for himself as an adult cartoonist as well as a children's author, wrote to ask Keats to write a few paragraphs for a new addition to his book *It's Fun Learning to Cartoon with Syd Hoff*. In a chatty letter, Syd promised to share the wealth for a double-page spread to the extent of twenty dollars. Citing Keats's appearance on *Mister*

Rogers' Neighborhood, he suggests that Keats get his own National Educational Television program in which he introduces a different book artist or author each week. He closes the letter with his unlisted number and his need to attend to his wife's yelling because he had been hammering away at the book all morning.

Keats's scribbled contribution noted his beginnings at the age of four drawing on paper bags, the sidewalk, or anything else that was handy. He added that he taught himself by reading books and going to the library and museums, and he gave credit to Syd Hoff, who made him laugh and understand his surroundings. In his following letter, Syd asked for permission to save Keats's contribution for another book that he was trying to sell on cartooning for younger children.

Macmillan, in some cost-cutting measures, brought a new issue that raised Keats's ire. The news was reported in a couple of articles, one called "The 1974 Macmillan Massacre" on the front page of the *New York Times* by Janet Schulman, who was marketing director at the time, and a *Washington Post* story headlined "Mac the Knife." Macmillan coped with their financial trouble by ordering respected editor Susan Hirschman to cut her author list in half, to fire four from her editorial staff of ten, and to eliminate three from her art department.

When Macmillan ignored her counterproposal, she and her associate editor, Ada Shearon, resigned in protest. Hirschman would be hired by Morrow the next year to begin a new children's division called Greenwillow Books. Keats joined those who picketed the company and wrote them a letter expressing his dismay and vowing that their children's editors formed "one of the finest juvenile book departments I have ever had the privilege of working for."

The Society of Children's Book Writers, in 1977 before it became the Society of Children's Book Writers and Illustrators,

invited Keats to lead two hour-long sessions at its annual meeting, the first on "Writing Picture Books" and the second in a question and answer format, for which they paid five hundred dollars
plus expenses. Stephen Mooser, one of the society's founders,
listed him as one of the early contributors when the organization
began and remembered that he was funny, warm, and generous.

After his books were translated into many languages, Keats
took trips to countries around the world. He enjoyed travels to
Europe, Egypt, and Iran. He made a special trip to Israel with his
high school teacher Florence Freedman. A trip to Copenhagen
and a visit to the Museum of the Resistance showed him courage
and resourcefulness he had not known as he admired King Christian, in an apocryphal story, leading his people to join the Jews
in donning yellow stars when Nazis ordered them to be worn.
The museum also triggered a memory he could not forget. When
he looked in a glass case and saw a threadbare herringbone coat
punctured by machine-gun bullets, he knew it had been worn
by a hero. He recalled the policeman pulling off his father's coat,
another working man who used safety pins to attach newspapers
to the lining of his own threadbare coat.

Having discovered that he could make a speech without a
pill for help, Keats enjoyed speaking to audiences of adults or
children all across the United States and in many other countries.
Everywhere he went, he signed autographs and talked to kids. No
matter how many honors and awards he received, Keats seemed
to enjoy his time with children the most. Friends noticed that
he didn't just talk to children but listened to what they had to
say as well. He never forgot his childhood longings for people
to pay heed to him.

Keats received many other honors for his work and books. He
was made an honorary citizen of Morgan City and Patterson in
Louisiana and mayor for the day in Fort Collins, Colorado. He

was the guest of honor at the International Festival of Films for Children in Tehran, Iran.

One special trip took him to the American Northwest, a new area for his travels, where he visited several schools and had a surprise parade in his honor planned by parents, librarians, and teachers with "hundreds and hundreds of children" dressed in costumes as characters from his books. No matter where he traveled, Keats received letters from Itch and Lillie. When Keats returned home to New York City from his travels, his appointment book might read, "F. Freedman." Often it said, "Lunch with Itch."

Between trips, Keats returned to his studio. Surrounded by toys from around the world, pictures drawn for him by children, and the plants and ferns he grew on windowsills and shelves, he welcomed time to return to the work he loved with only his cat Samantha to supervise.

Through the years, Keats had worried about his health and his finances. He had visited therapists off and on, some offering more help than others. He tried Seconal and drifted in and out of relationships with women. None of these gave him the consistent satisfaction he found in writing his books for children and interacting with them. Those books and the recognition they brought gave voice to the little boy unnoticed at the dinner table.

Keats enjoyed what he perceived as secret celebrity, in which people find that you mean something to them, not because they've seen you on TV but because you have touched children's lives. Grown-up kids and teenagers who once read his books met him with delight. Teachers and librarians, part of that private world of children, considered him a pied piper. He loved knowing that millions of kids remembered his books with delight. "Dear Mr. Keats," one wrote, "We like you because you have the mind of a child."

He used his platform to advocate for children:

Most adults don't know what it's like to be a creator of children's books. In touch with children. The world we live in that parents don't know about. Like what grows under trees—mushrooms—truffles—you have to reach for them. Prizes.

Parents live out their lives well intentioned—send them to school—buying them books, toys, clothing, food—what else is there to care about?

Continuing his didacticism, he took both parents and the education system to task for its structure and predictability, saying that American parents were missing the key and teaching was done by rote. "Storybooks, happily are often so unfettered, unpredictable, however subtly, release you into new areas of feelings, sympathies and connections."

He felt that the children in his books had made him a parent as they grew, experiencing joy, struggle, fear, and success. He had watched them grow and sent them out into the world. "Like any parent," he said, "it hasn't been all beer and skittles," but good things happened, and his books appeared in countries around the world. His books reflected childhood as he thought it should be, often reminiscent of his own but idealized into a better form.

With world travels and a lifetime mix of struggle and adventure behind him, Ezra Jack Keats became a raconteur, entertaining friends at dinner parties. He fascinated students and teachers on school visits, spoke to appreciative audiences at book festivals, and wrote his stories for educational journals and for *Horn Book Magazine*. Looking back, he reminisced about his birth to Jewish immigrant parents, a sickly childhood, a stressful adolescence during the Great Depression, and adversities as a young artist. He wondered at his own transformation into an award-winning, sought-after writer, speaker, and world traveler. Experiences from those difficult early days wound their way into his children's books. Audiences at his formal lectures or around dinner tables responded appreciatively when he told tales from his present interactions with children and recounted stories from his past seasoned with insights on childhood. The adult Keats combined a love for children with a compulsion to shed light for adults on how they were to be treated.

In his speeches to various groups and in magazine articles, his personal story came to the forefront. He decided that maybe a publisher would be interested in his autobiography.

Herman Goliob, an editor at Atheneum Publishers, responded to this suggestion in a letter dated 17 May 1974:

> Dear Mr. Keats,
>
> Those autobiographical fragments you gave me the other day were moving, disturbing, and evocative. Could I see more of the manuscript, or could you at least give me a notion of what you see as the general shape of the book?
>
> Sincerely,
>
> Herman Goliob

There are no other letters with the editor in his files, but an encouraged Keats began to write and shared his hope of getting the book published. His autobiography is mentioned in a November 1976 letter from Mrs. Takako Nishinoya, editor at the Kaisei-Sha Publishing Company: "Mrs. Ishitake who has returned from your country had told me that you are now starting for your biography which pleased me very much."

In a 2 January 1981 letter, Beverly Hall, who took the photographs of him over the years and for his selections in *Night*, reflected on fifteen years of memorabilia, including the most intimate: an x-ray of his ankle. Evidently responding to a request related to the autobiography he was attempting, she stressed this would be the most important work he could do this year and volunteered to contribute if he needed someone else's opinion of him.

Early chapters of the autobiography were hard to write, bringing memories drawn from eavesdropping on his parents' arguments, vignettes at family gatherings, and overheard conversations in his community of immigrants.

One night, Keats began to write an account of a more pleasant but well-remembered incident, relishing every detail of the exciting turning point when he was in junior high school and discovered the Arlington Branch Public Library. He saw himself wandering out of his tenement neighborhood in Brooklyn into other streets with fancy houses and ancient trees and discovering the library at the end of his stroll, nestled in the midst of this elite community with people going in and out. He wanted to see it again to be sure his narrative was right.

Questions from the night's writing about discovering the library inundated his mind and brought him fully awake early the next morning. "Would that library still be there? Would those same houses and overhanging trees still surround it? Would it still have those special steps inside leading up to the art books? Would the long tables be there where he had spread the books to study technique and teach himself to paint?"

The clock said 4:00 AM, much too early to go in search of answers. Daylight came slowly until, finally, he decided the library must be open. Taking the trek down the familiar street, he passed the houses, a bit more worn and not as elaborate as he remembered, until there it was, shadowed by the old trees: the Arlington Branch of the Brooklyn Public Library. Apparently, Keats had not waited long enough, for the library remained locked. He banged on the door to get attention until someone inside motioned to him and mouthed, "We're not open yet."

Keats's lifetime dream started in this red brick building with its stone masonry trim, but so much had changed. His children's books had won awards and been published in sixteen languages. He had traveled the world, but now he really must see inside. Would they still have his old beloved art books? Better yet, would his own books be there?

Taking the trip back to see if his memory was accurate, he was in no mood to be denied entrance. When Keats saw the librarian signal, "We're closed," he only knocked harder. Finally, she opened a crack in the door. Keats explained that he was writing about the library, and he needed to see inside.

The librarian let him in. As he looked around, he felt like he was fourteen years old again: the library had the same shelves, the same books, and the same electric fans. He recognized the windows with trees pressing against them as if they were reaching out to grab him.

Keats saw the familiar stairway with its "Reference Room" riser. Walking up softly, he came to the loft room on one side with the long tables where he had spread the big art books that he couldn't take home. How simple it had seemed to decide that he would become an artist.

Keats returned to the main floor and crossed to the other side of the library. Another staircase that he didn't remember led to a different loft room. Its riser said, "Children's Room." Maybe by the time he'd discovered the library, he had thought he was too old for these books. Or could it be he had not noticed because no one in his childhood neighborhood knew much about children's books?

Walking up the steps, he thought about his own books. "Would they be there?" He hurried and found the shelves with all his friends—Peter, Louie, Amy, Willie, Clementine, and Archie. Keats gazed in wonder. He believed his life journey began with the staircase to the art in the reference room and now had circled back to the other staircase with his books featured in the children's room. He was sure the boy Jacob Ezra Katz would have been amazed at the long and winding pathway that had led him to become the author Ezra Jack Keats.

Perhaps Keats hoped that the example of his own journey from poverty to a satisfying and influential career would be inspirational. Whatever his motivation, his premature death left the autobiography unfinished.

Keats continued to worry about his health and finances, sometimes with reason. Often, as Ezra walked Itch back to work, they discussed his ongoing sinus and ulcer problems, the development of his severe heart trouble, and his book business. Ezra's feelings for his friend had changed only by growing stronger since they had walked each other home when they were boys. He consulted Itch about what foods he should eat, his ideas for promoting his book with a publicity firm, and a new series of activity books for younger children. In one of their conversations, Ezra told Itch he wanted to establish a foundation that would use the royalties from his books to "do good." In 1964, the Ezra Jack Keats Foundation was incorporated, with Ezra as president and Martin as secretary, but it would remain private until after his death.

Keats also worried that all his books would go out of print, leaving him without money for food and rent. Worry about his health was warranted; worry about the demise of his books was unnecessary.

Keats's weak heart, perhaps an inheritance from his parents, caused him to cancel a February visit planned by Dr. Patsy Perritt to speak at Louisiana State University in order to have double bypass surgery in 1980. He recovered in time to receive a significant honor in April, when the School of Library Services at the University of Southern Mississippi presented him with their annual Medallion for distinguished contributions to children's literature. The author/illustrator bonded with the Mississippi librarians and invited them to visit him in Brooklyn. Conversations about the care of his archives ensued, with an ultimate decision to place them in the de Grummond Children's Literature Collection at the university. His incomplete autobiography is included in those archives.

Two years later, Ezra Jack Keats died on 6 May 1983. His friend Martin Pope stood at his bedside holding his hand. Martin looked up and saw city skyscrapers and water towers silhouetted against an orange and purple sky, just as Keats had painted in his books. He thought, "Ezra is walking me home."

$\mathscr{A}$FTERWORD

MARTIN POPE HAD INSTRUCTIONS IN KEATS'S WILL FOR HIS interment. Keats requested that his body lie in state for three days after his death to allow friends to attend the funeral and designated a nonreligious service with Martin to select the speakers and include himself. Afterward, he wanted his body cremated and the ashes scattered to the winds.

The Ezra Jack Keats Foundation, incorporated in 1964, had remained private, with Ezra as president and his friend Martin as secretary until his death. His will directed that the Foundation would use the royalties from his books to do social good. The completion of that directive would fall to his old friends Doctors Martin and Lillie Pope, a team both in their leadership and in their commitment to Keats's lifework and dreams. Their life experiences made them ideally suited to the task.

Dr. Martin Pope had followed his childhood bent in science to become a professor at New York University and director of its Radiation and Solid State Physics Lab. He became known for his pioneering work in electroluminescence and for invention of techniques used to study organic materials. Dr. Lillie Pope, equally prominent in her chosen field of education as founding director of the Learning and Reading Disabilities Program at Coney Island Hospital in Brooklyn, developed a reading program that served as a model for others and authored books and tests on reading education. Her expertise in mental health, reading instruction, and special education made her the logical choice to design the Foundation's core programs.

In the ensuing years, the Pope family has administered the Foundation, focusing on the children who were so important to Keats. Remembering that public schools and libraries in his impoverished childhood were the inspiration and means for his ultimate success, the Foundation seeks through those same institutions to give new generations of children similar opportunities to establish belief in themselves and a love of reading and learning. The Foundation's work promotes Keats's ideals of the common qualities of childhood, the importance of family, and the multicultural nature of the world. It has fulfilled his desire to do social good to an extent that probably would have astonished Keats.

In an early program to establish an international award for beginning illustrators in keeping with Keats's themes, the Foundation teamed with the UNICEF and the US Books for Young Children (USBBY). The first award went to Felipe Davolos in June 1986 for his work in *Las Tortugas de Mar* (Turtles of the Sea) and *Un Asalto Mayusculo* (A Capital Assault). The first award was limited to newly published children's book illustrators in Canada, Mexico, and the United States. The award, which was later suspended as UNICEF underwent a reorganization, became international and was part of a worldwide broadcast from The Hague hosted by Audrey Hepburn in 1992.

Hannah Nuba proposed the creation of an Ezra Jack Keats Book Award as a collaboration between the New York Public

Library and the Foundation, to be chosen by an independent panel of scholars, teachers, librarians, authors, and illustrators. The first winner was Valerie Flournoy for her book *The Patchwork Quilt* in 1985. Bryan Collier became the first New Illustrator winner for his book *Uptown*, when that award was added in 2001. Honor categories, inaugurated in 2012, give recognition to a wider group of beginning artists and writers.

With these Writer and Illustrator Awards and Honor Book Awards each year for books demonstrating Keats's ideals, the Foundation encourages word and picture artists at the beginning of their careers. Many of these talented artists have gone on to make their mark in the world of children's literature, writing and illustrating books that have won other prestigious awards, including the Newbery Medal and the Caldecott Award. Significantly, Sophie Blackall, who won the 2019 Caldecott Award for *Hello, Lighthouse*, and Meg Medina, who won the 2019 Newbery Award for *Merci Suarez Changes Gears*, were both Ezra Jack Keats Award winners early in their careers.

The Popes have maintained the relationship with the University of Southern Mississippi begun in Keats's lifetime, with regular attendance at its annual Faye B. Kaigler Children's Book Festival and annual sponsorship of a Keats lecturer for one of its presentations. In 2012, the Ezra Jack Keats Awards ceremony for new writers and illustrators was moved to the festival and has become an anticipated feature of the event with a Keats luncheon and an evening reception in the renovated Hattiesburg depot.

Dr. Deborah Pope, daughter of Martin and Lillie, added a new dimension when she became executive director of the Foundation in 1999. With her extensive background in theater and arts in education, she brought a mission of expanding existing parts of the program to many beneficiaries, as illustrated by her advancement of two programs begun in 1986.

Initially instituted with a partnership with the New York City Department of Education, students from grades three through twelve examine the picture book genre and create their own books under the supervision of visual arts teachers, English teachers, and librarians for the Ezra Jack Keats Bookmaking Competition. An award winner, selected from each school, goes on to be judged for their borough and the citywide competition with all participants' creations displayed in their schools. Demonstrated success of the program lies in the total number of student-created books, enough to fill a small library, and in the program expansion to the cities of San Francisco and Atlanta.

The Ezra Jack Keats minigrant program, open to public schools, libraries, and preschool programs such as Head Start, provides up to seventy awards yearly for innovative programs that support basic education standards. Fittingly honoring the founder of the Foundation and his passions, chosen projects provide an enriched learning experience through the arts, with more than one million dollars given to educators at public schools and libraries since 1987. Under Deborah Pope's leadership, application forms have been simplified and publicity increased with all needed information and forms on the Foundation's website. The website also gives resources for families, educators, and researchers; games for children based on Keats's books; and information about other ongoing and special programs.

Taking advantage of her theatrical background, Deborah wrote and served as executive producer of an Amazon Original animated holiday special of *The Snowy Day*, premiering in 2016, that won two Daytime Emmys for Outstanding Preschool Children's Animated Program and for Music Direction and Composition.

Another of her campaigns paid off when the US Postal Service issued four *Snowy Day* stamps in 2017 featuring Peter playing in the snow. Renowned artist Antonio Alcalá designed the stamps showing Peter sledding and making snowballs, snow angels, and tracks in the snow. Appropriately, the first day of celebration for the issue was held at the Brooklyn Public Library with wide media publicity.

Ron Charles, book critic for the *Washington Post*, responded to the issuance of the stamps and looked back to his own childhood in an article that proposed that *The Snowy Day* on a postage stamp might help us rethink race in America. He noted that while he grew up in a "blindingly white suburb" of St. Louis and did not know any African Americans, his parents read books to him and introduced him to Peter. He posits that while the stamps probably will not change any minds or pass legislation, they will remind former child readers of the boy they met. He notes a metaphor in the fact that these are "forever" stamps.

Other groups and individuals separately and in conjunction with the Keats Foundation have contributed to continuing Keats's legacy.

The *New York Times* reviewed the play based on *The Trip* in its Sunday, 11 December 1983 edition: "The charm of this very simple tale develops in part from the fact that Mr. Keats, who died shortly before the show opened, designed the sets and the costumes from his own drawings for the book, so the visual quality is transferred to the stage with no change in point of view."

Prospect Park Alliance commissioned sculptor Otto Neals to create an artwork for children to inspire their imaginations. The sculpture of Peter and his beloved dog Willie was dedicated in 1997 and won the New York City Art Commission Award for Design Excellence and on 10 June 2016 was honored by United for Libraries with a plaque from the New York City Parks Department as an honorary Literary Landmark.

Bryan Collier opened his keynote address to the summer meeting of the Society of Children's Book Writers and Illustrators

Summer Conference on 3 August 2012: "When I was a little boy, my mother taught Head Start. She brought home *Harold and the Purple Crayon* and *The Snowy Day*, and for the first time, I saw myself in a picture book. I never met him (Keats) but when he put Peter in the book, he spoke just to me."

He thought the dress Peter's mother wore was similar to one of his mother's housedresses and the pattern of Peter's pajamas like his great-uncle's. Now an acclaimed children's book illustrator, Collier's first book, *Uptown*, coincidentally winner of the first Ezra Jack Keats New Illustrator Award, carries a tribute to Keats in the traffic light modeled after the one Peter leans against in *The Snowy Day*.

A yearlong observation of the fiftieth anniversary of the first publication of *The Snowy Day* came with a special edition produced by Viking with eight supplementary pages gleaned from the Keats archives. Claudia Nahson, curator of New York's Jewish Museum, organized an exhibit about Keats that opened in New York in the fall of 2012. Her research in the de Grummond Children's Literature Collection archives for display items also informed her book with an essay by Maurice Berger, published by Yale University Press in conjunction with the exhibition, *The Snowy Day and the Art of Ezra Jack Keats*. The exhibit traveled to the Eric Carle Museum in Amherst, Massachusetts, in 2012 and on to the Contemporary Jewish Museum in San Francisco, California, and to the Akron Art Museum in Ohio in 2013.

Eric Carle, in his introduction to the Keats exhibit at the Eric Carle Museum of Picture Book Art in 2012, recalled Keats's influence on his own work. In the mid-1960s as he began his work as an illustrator, a friend offered to introduce him to Keats. Soon after, they had lunch together and Keats invited him to his studio to show his marbleized papers. Their conversation moved into the business of publishing, and Keats assured the beginning illustrator that a living could be made from illustrating children's books. The development from strangers to colleagues to friends left Carle grateful for the professional who had reached out to him with such a kind and generous spirit.

The day 2 June 2015 saw Keats inducted into the New York State Hall of Fame, established by the Empire State Center for the Book to highlight the rich literary heritage of the state and to recognize the literary legacy of individual writers. His name joined other notable writers such as Isaac Asimov, David Remick, and Allen Ginsberg and previous winners like Walt Whitman, Joyce Carol Oates, and Toni Morrison.

Keats and *The Snowy Day* have become and remain part of the common culture. Michelle Obama answered a question about favorite books in a *New York Times* interview after the publication of her memoir: "So once I had kids of my own, I liked to find characters who looked like my girls—but at the same time the stories didn't have to be centered on race. One of our favorites was *The Snowy Day* by Ezra Jack Keats."

Michelle H. Martin, in an article promoting the importance of seeing African American children in the outdoors in the September/October 2019 issue of *Horn Book Magazine*, lists *The Snowy Day* as one of only three picture books she has found that embrace this "wildness." In her take on the book, she says, "*The Snowy Day* paints a picture of a Black kid immersed in his enjoyment of the outdoors long before other white writers and illustrators of Keats's time saw a need for this portrayal."

Keats's reality has been contrary to Shakespearean wisdom, "The good men do is often interred in their bones." In the years following his death, the world of child advocates has taken notice of Keats's connection to children and unwittingly fulfilled his longing, held over from this ex-kid's childhood, to be heard.

Benjamin Katz, Keats's father, came to the United States in 1883 as an orphan, shuffled from one uncle in Poland to another uncle in America. Used with permission from the Ezra Jack Keats Foundation.

Augusta Katz, Keats's mother, came to the United States at age thirteen with her Podgaisky family when they fled the pogroms in Poland. Used with permission from the Ezra Jack Keats Foundation.

Keats's painting of his parents in the style of Daumier caused trouble for him with his family and their friends. Used with permission from the de Grummond Children's Literature Collection, University of Southern Mississippi.

Keats at sixteen was already winning awards for his art. Used with permission from the Ezra Jack Keats Foundation.

Jack Katz's painting *Shantytown* won first place in a national competition sponsored by the Carnegie Foundation. Used with permission from the de Grummond Children's Literature Collection, University of Southern Mississippi.

WINS NATIONAL SCHOLASTIC ART PRIZE.

"Shantytown," by Jack Katz, a student of the Thomas Jefferson High School in Brooklyn, who was awarded first place in oils in the competition sponsored by Scholastic, the national high school with the support of the Carnegie Corporation of New York.

SCHOLASTIC PRIZES IN THE ARTS LISTED

Philadelphia Boy Gets Most Awards in National Art and Literature Competition.

NEW YORKERS WIN PLACES

Detroit and Pittsburgh Tie for Single School Honors—700 Cities Represented.

Winners of the 1934 scholastic awards for creative work by secondary students in art and literature were announced yesterday by Scholastic, national high school weekly, which sponsors the awards with the support of the Carnegie Corporation of New York.

According to the announcement, secondary schools of more than 700 towns and cities entered the art competition held at Carnegie Institute, Pittsburgh, and the total value of the scholastic awards was more than $10,000.

The highest number of awards was won by Jacob Landau, 16 years old, of Overbrook High School, Philadelphia, who received one first place, two seconds, one third and one fourth place in five separate pictorial competitions.

The Cass Tech School in Detroit, which has for several years led all other secondary schools in the art competition, was tied for first honors this year by students of Connelley Trade School, Pittsburgh. West Tech School of Cleveland was third.

Of the schools which do not give full time to art studies, Alhambra (Cal.) High School, Norwich (Conn.) Free Academy and Washington Irving High School, New York, were announced as best represented.

Schools excelling in literary work were Stivers High School, Dayton, Ohio, with two firsts and a fourth; University High School, Oakland, Calif., with first in poetry and third in drama; Tucson (Ariz.) High School, whose students took five minor honors; Peekskill (N. Y.) High School, Oak Park (Ill.) Township High School and West High School, Seattle, Wash.

Highest literary honors were won by:

Short Story—Grace Hembel, 18, West Bend (Wis.) High School, $50.
Poetry—Joyce Hoeft, 17, University High School, Oakland, Cal., $50.
Essay—Louise Cooper, 17, Stivers High School, Dayton, Ohio, $50.
Drama—Betty Fitzgerald, 16, Missoula (Mont.) High School, $25.

Scholarships to art schools were awarded the following students:

To the Art Institute of Chicago—Robert Alvin White, Arsenal Technical Schools, Indianapolis.
To Carnegie Institute of Technology, Pittsburgh—Bob Evans, Austin High School, El Paso, Texas.
To Vesper George School of Art, Boston—John Lowrey Farrell, Free Academy, Norwich, Conn.
To Columbus School of Art, Columbus, Ohio—Gertrude Goodrich, Washington Irving High School, New York City.
To Pratt Institute, Brooklyn—James A. Ernst, Hastings-On-Hudson High School, Hastings-On-Hudson, N. Y.
To California School of Art—Oakland, Cal.—Eleanor Anne High School, St...
To Fort Wayne...

... School, Lakewood, Ohio.
To Moore Institute of Art, Science, Industry, Philadelphia—Alvina Beckar, High School, Allentown, Pa.
To Art School of the Detroit Society of Arts and Crafts, Detroit—Hughie L. Smith, East Tech High School, Cleveland.
To Dayton Art Institute, Dayton, Ohio—Alphonse B. Sacs, High School, Huntington, L. I.
To Rudolf Schaeffer Studios School of Rhythmo-Chromatic Design, San Francisco—Richard Bird, North Central High School, Spokane, Wash.
To California School of Arts and Crafts (Summer session), Oakland, Calif.—Alma Reddekopp, Garfield High School, Seattle, Wash.

Some of the awards in New York were:

Manhattan and Bronx.

Penmanship Prizes—Winifred Byles, Female Academy of the Sacred Heart; John Joseph Bahre, La Salle Academy; Murray Hartman, Morris High School.
Drama—Edward Watkins, 17, Theodore Roosevelt High School, fourth place, $2.50, for "Sometimes They Die."
George Bellows Memorial Awards — Irving Graff, 17, Boys High School, fourth place, $2.50.
Sculpture—Raphael Epstein, 17, Commerce High School, fourth place, $2.50.
Prints—Jack Weinstein, 18, De Witt Clinton High School, fourth place, $2.50.
Design—Janet Boxley, 18, fourth place, $2.50; May Krisl, 16, second place, $25; Alice Kyriacou, 15, fourth place, $2.50; Nadja D. Pashkovsky, 16, fourth place, $2.50, all of Washington Irving High School.

Brooklyn.

Sculpture—Daniel Miller, 15, Boys High School, fourth place, $2.50.
Oils—Jack Katz, 19, Jefferson High School, first place, $30; Angelo Spadaro, 17, Lincoln High School, fourth place.
Prints—Anthony D'Esposito, 18, Lincoln High School, fourth place, $2.50.
Penmanship—Clara Myash, Bay Ridge High School.
Drama—Edward R. McCann, 19, Alexander Hamilton High School, second place, $15; drama, "Venus D. Miller."
Poetry—Miriam Hershenson, fourth place, $5, and Henry Terman, fourth place, $5, both of Thomas Jefferson High School.
Book Review—Helen Hudesman, 15, Samuel J. Tilden High School, fourth place.

Staten Island.

Carnegie Museum Awards—Pauline Miller, 17, fourth place, $2.50; Nedra Wilson, 17, second place, $15, both of Notre Dame Convent.
Book Review—Hume Dow, 18, Staten Island Academy, first place, $15.

Jack Katz, in his early career, worked as part of a team of comic book artists, moving up from a "fill-in" position to drawing characters. Used with permission from the de Grummond Children's Literature Collection, University of Southern Mississippi.

Corporal Jack Katz in Tampa during World War II. Used with permission from the de Grummond Children's Literature Collection, University of Southern Mississippi.

A watercolor produced during a year in Paris when Jack was adrift after World War II. Used with permission from the de Grummond Children's Literature Collection, University of Southern Mississippi.

My Dog Is Lost, the first book in which Keats had the option of choosing the characters, is populated with the rich diversity represented in New York neighborhoods. Used with permission from the de Grummond Children's Literature Collection, University of Southern Mississippi.

Keats in the 1950s taught art classes and did freelance art for magazines, advertising, and other people's book jackets and books. Used with permission from the Ezra Jack Keats Foundation.

Keats in the 1960s came into his own as he became the author and illustrator of an abundance of children's books. Used with permission from the Ezra Jack Keats Foundation.

PICTURES TO THE EDITORS
(continued)

BLOOD TEST

Sirs:

—This little Negro boy was at school in Liberty County, Ga. the day a State Health Officer and Health Nurse came to take blood tests of the schoolchildren for a malaria survey. His reaction to the blood test is shown in the pictures.

EDNA CAIN DANIEL
Quitman Free Press
Quitman, Ga.

CHILD IS CAREFREE AT FIRST

HE ASKS IF TEST WILL HURT

TRUSTINGLY HE HOLDS OUT HAND

TEST HURT AND HE STARTS TO CRY

LANGSTON HUGHES
20 EAST 127TH STREET
NEW YORK 35, N. Y.

February 18, 1963

Dear Miss Crittenden:

THE SNOWY DAY by Ezra Jack Keats is a perfectly charming little book. I wish I had some grandchildren to give it to. Yes, I do!

Sincerely yours,

Langston Hughes

Langston Hughes

Keats was thrilled with this letter that was passed along to him from Langston Hughes, leader in the Harlem Renaissance. Used with permission from the de Grummond Children's Literature Collection, University of Southern Mississippi.

In his first book, *The Snowy Day*, Keats used a picture of a boy for his model that he had saved from a *Life* magazine clipping some twenty years before. Used with permission from the de Grummond Children's Literature Collection, University of Southern Mississippi.

One of many parades honoring Keats and his books. Used with permission from the de Grummond Children's Literature Collection, University of Southern Mississippi.

Keats enjoyed these parades as much as the children. Used with permission from the de Grummond Children's Literature Collection, University of Southern Mississippi.

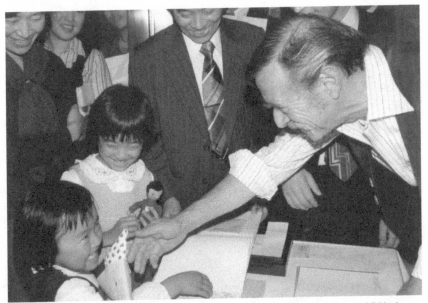

Keats became known for connecting with children wherever he went. Used with permission from the de Grummond Children's Literature Collection, University of Southern Mississippi.

Hand cramps were the only problem Keats found in the book signings. Used with permission from the de Grummond Children's Literature Collection, University of Southern Mississippi.

The Ohanashi Caravan planned Keats's tour in Japan in 1973. Used with permission from the de Grummond Children's Literature Collection, University of Southern Mississippi.

Keats book *Skates!* became the impetus for a skating rink named for him that Keats opened on a visit. Used with permission from the de Grummond Children's Literature Collection, University of Southern Mississippi.

The big celebration to open the skating rink brought Keats back to Japan and found many of his fans ready to try out their skates. Used with permission from the de Grummond Children's Literature Collection, University of Southern Mississippi.

Keats, following Buddhist tradition, honors the grave of his young fan Akira Ishida. Used with permission from the de Grummond Children's Literature Collection, University of Southern Mississippi.

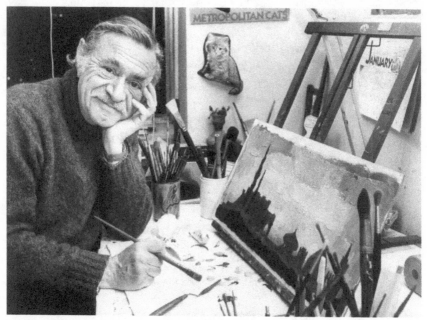

By the 1980s, Keats's studio felt like a home populated with children who told him stories to include in his next book. Used with permission from the Ezra Jack Keats Foundation.

The Arlington Branch of the Brooklyn Public Library, built with funds from Andrew Carnegie, remains largely unchanged from its original classical revival structure. Finding this library when he was in junior high school was a defining point in Keats's life. Photograph courtesy of Lauren Damaskinos.

Young Ezra Katz took this staircase to the reference loft of the library, where he taught himself art by reading all the art books. Photograph courtesy of Lauren Damaskinos.

Near the end of his life, Ezra Jack Keats returned to the library and took the opposite staircase to find his books in the children's loft. Photograph courtesy of Lauren Damaskinos.

$\mathcal{A}$CKNOWLEDGMENTS

THIS BOOK WOULD NOT EXIST WITHOUT THE HELP AND SUP-port of many people. First of all, there was Ezra Jack Keats himself, a master storyteller whose own life was one of his favorite sub-jects. His most detailed account resides in the many drafts of his unfinished autobiography in his archives at the de Grummond Children's Literature Collection at the University of Southern Mississippi (USM). I thank him for being a collector who saved everything from notable awards to newspaper clippings to lunch receipts. In Ezra's account, he says he became acquainted with his young friend Akira Ishida after his death. I thought, "Ezra, I know exactly what you mean."

The Ezra Jack Keats Foundation and its director, Dr. Deborah Pope, along with the de Grummond Children's Literature Col-lection and its curator, Ellen Ruffin, have given generous access and several incentives for me to delve into the rich Keats archives along with encouragement to tell Ezra's story. The Special Collec-tions Staff in the Brooke Reading Room at the McCain Library of USM saved my favorite table, kept my research cart full, and listened with real or well-feigned interest when I discovered exciting Keats nuggets.

Editor Katie Keene shared my vision for *Becoming Ezra Jack Keats* from my first contact with her. Subsequently, the University Press of Mississippi team has put untiring effort into polishing, copyediting, and promotional support. I am grateful for their hard work and for their unfailing encouragement in the process.

The late Jerry Shepherd of Main Street Books in Hattiesburg found copies of all of the books that Keats both wrote and illustrated, as well as some he only illustrated, for my personal collection so I would have them at hand while I wrote.

The coronavirus pandemic brought Louisiana lagniappe of partnership with the 7Cz Critique Group, which meet twice a week via Zoom. They have read my manuscript with a balance of friendship and nitpicking, fretting over comma placement and word choice as if the writing were their own. Beta readers, Dr. Patricia Austin and Gena Lott, also gave great attention to details.

I thank my family for their encouragement and for refraining from rolling their eyes at yet another mention of Keats. A special thanks goes to photographer granddaughter, Lauren Damaskinos, for her care in taking the pictures of the Arlington Branch Public Library that meant so much to Keats, and to my husband, Al, who took care of routine tasks to give me time to write.

Source Notes

Abbreviations used in the Notes

BT—Ezra Jack Keats biography tapes held in the de Grummond Children's Literature
    Collection
CF—Ezra Jack Keats correspondence files held in the de Grummond Children's
    Literature Collection
FF—Ezra Jack Keats file folders held in the de Grummond Children's Literature
    Collection
FW—Ezra Jack Keats Foundation website

Page numbers are noted unless there were none.

CHAPTER 1. SHAKY START: ART AND ILLNESS

3	"I really am . . . good memory." FF 60.07, *Minneapolis Star*, 26 Oct. 1966.
4	"Jacob Ezra Katz . . . scrawny baby." BT 76.05.
4	"who remained . . . he is!" FF 70.01, 5.
4	"Ezra always remembered . . . went to sleep." BT 76.05; FF 71.22, 3.
4	"Ezra claimed . . . his first paintings." FF 70.01, 1.
5	"Ezra's orphaned father . . . to America." FF 70.19, 20.
5	"His mother Augusta's . . . everybody left." BT 76.04; FF 76.05.
5	"Needing to find safety . . . May 5, 1891." "Immigration Photos and Pictures." Accessed 5 July 2011, www.maggieblanck.com/Immigration.html.
5–6	"These immigrants bought . . . their scant meals." H. Phelps Whitmarsh. "Steerage Conditions in 1898—A First-Hand Account." Accessed 5 July 2011,

www.gjenvick.com/Steerage/1898-SteerageConditions-A Personal Experience.html; "Immigration Photos and Pictures."

6   "A sailor took pity . . . peel and all." FF 75.09, 10.

6   "With the steerage . . . immigrant vessels." "The Crossing."

6   "Jenny did not live . . . voyage." FF 75.09, 10.

6   "Their ship landed . . . return journey." "Immigration Photos and Pictures."

6   "After the family had . . . had vouched for them." FF 75.09, 10.

6   "Thirteen-year-old . . . not a word of English." FF 70.19, 20.

6–7   "Both the Katz . . . store." FF 73.22; 75.09.

7   "Choices for . . . church." FF 70.19, 8.

7   "There was . . . errands." FF 73.22, 2.

7   "These immigrant . . . each other." FF 70.19, 6.

7   "They settled . . . children." BT 76.05.

7   "Gussie and . . . his life." FF 75.03, 3.

7–8   "When he was . . . off the table." BT 76.05; 70.01, 1–2.

9   "Often, Ezra's stomach . . . he cried." BT 76.04.

9   "Once he had to . . . home again." FF 86.17, Florence Freedman, "Brochure of Ezra Jack Keats." Reprinted from *Elementary English*, Jan. 1969, 56.

CHAPTER 2. AT HOME AND SCHOOL

10   "Ezra used his . . . prison walls." BT 76.05; FF 74.28, 2.

11   "Another change . . . the paper." FF 74.18, 9.

11   "Ezra copied . . . drawings." BT 76.05.

11   "Two teachers . . . Mrs. Houghton." BT 76.05; FF 74.22, 45.

11–12   "A happier memory . . . by his art." BT 76.05; FF 74.17, 7; 74.18, 5.

12   "At home . . . people who sew." BT 76.01; FF 70.23, 17.

12–13   "There were no . . . set it again." FF 75.03, 24.

13   "Perhaps what Ezra . . . himself." BT 76.04; FF 74.23, 23.

13   "At one time . . . him away." BT 76.04; FF 70.03, 8.

13–14   "Yom Kippur . . . went down." BT 76.

14   "Because he worked . . . a yarn." FF 76.01, 1–8.

14–15   "Sometimes when . . . and sleep." BT 76.05.

15   "The Katz family . . . hard times." BT 76.05; FF 70.16, 1; 70.19, 2.

15   "Ezra envied . . . crying spells." BT 76.04; FF 70.19, 3–7.

15–16   "By the time . . . give you." FF 70.12, 4.

16   "Uncle Louie . . . for him!" FF 70.12, 5; 70.20, 7–12.

16–19   "He's wasting away . . . They waited." BT 76.04; FF 70.12, 5–7; 70.20, 7–12.

19   "The sorrow . . . whipped cream." FF 70.23, 8.

19–20 "His parents' worry . . . into his paintings." BT 76.02; 76.08; FF 70.01, 2; 70.04, 1–4; 75.03, 24; 75.04, 3, 19.

20 "Sometimes his mother . . . already asleep." BT 76.08; FF 70.04, I–1.

20–21 "Sometimes Ezra's found . . . feeling guilty." BT 76.04; FF 74.24, 8.

21–26 "Uncle Louie . . . May I?" BT 76.04; 76.05; FF 70.06, 1–9.

26 "For many nights . . . fell back asleep." FF 70.19, 1.

26 "The crying spells stopped . . . nine." BT 76.07.

26 "controversy continued . . . the edges." BT 76.05; FF 74.18, 13.

26–27 "In the meantime . . . his art." FF 71.06, 2; 86.17, Freedman, "Brochure of Ezra Jack Keats," 56–57.

Note: Isaac Bashevis Singer, in his memoir *In My Father's Court* (New York: Farrar, Straus, and Giroux, 1966), gives an autobiographical account of a Good Jew and his family.

CHAPTER 3. LIFE ON VERMONT STREET

28 "Summer weather . . . a parachute." BT 76.05; FF 74.08, 1–2.

28–29 "Duddie exhibited . . . in a sea battle." FF 74.17, 1.

29 "Some boys . . . new scarfalife." FF 74.08, 2–3.

29–30 "Sometimes the . . . was repaired." FF 73.22, 2.

30 "Duddie and Ezra . . . own scarfalife." FF 74.18, 1.

30 "Neighborhood mothers . . . straggled home." FF 74.08, 7; 74.16, 1.

30 "Winter brought . . . white shapes." FF 75.09.

30–31 "Teddy, who . . . the movie." BT 76.08; FF 70.33, 3.

31 "One night . . . closer than ever." FF 70.27, 5; 70.33, 5–6.

31–32 "Ezra accidentally . . . with respect." FF 70.04, I–1.

32 "About this time . . . his art." BT 76.03; FF 75.01, 9.

33–34 "Sometimes Ezra . . . tiny bits." BT 76.02; FF 75.05, 1–2.

34–35 "Kids weren't the . . . zaddik's board." FF 70.19, 10–13; 74.08, 3–5.

35 "Nobody in . . . what 'It' was." FF 60.20, draft of speech for *Chicago Tribune* tribute; 86.17, Freedman, "Brochure of Ezra Jack Keats," 57.

35 "In his next . . . face." Dan P. Lee, "Peaches: Who's Your Daddy?" The History of New York Scandals—Peaches Browning's Acid Attack. *New York Magazine.* Accessed 17 Oct. 2018, http://nymag.com/news/features/scandals/peaches-browning-2012-4/index1.html.

35 "Knowing Daddy . . . house paints." FF 60.20, speech draft.

35–36 "Christmas time . . . all away." FF 74.16, 3–4.

36 "Young Ezra . . . celebrate." FF 70.19, 8.

36   "when Charles . . . 'Lucky Lindy.'" Norman H. Finklestein, *Three Across* (Honesdale, PA: Calkins Creek/Boyds Mills Press, 2008), 36, 45.

37   "With other . . . Paris." FF 74.18.

37   "They waited . . . Central Park." Finklestein, *Three Across*, 61–62.

37   "The Vermont . . . to do?" FF 74.18.

37–38   "The following year. . . . Jack E. Katz." CF Al Smith, letter dated 8 Oct. 1928.

CHAPTER 4. HARD CHANGES AND OPPORTUNITIES

39–40   "In another step . . . excellent cook." FF 74.22, 2–3.

40   "Even Ezra's Bar . . . tenement." BT 76.07; FF 70.21.

40   "But there were . . . friends' parents." FF 74.22, 2.

40   "His brother . . . casual conversation." BT 76.05; FF 74.14, 1–4; 75.01, 6–8.

40–41   "The best thing . . . his punishment." BT 76.02; FF 74.25, 3; Deborah Pope conversations with the author.

41   "The boys lived . . . formally." Martin and Lillie Pope, telephone conversation with the author, 8 July 2011.

41   "Enjoying their . . . it all." BT 76.02; FF 74.25, 3.

41–42   "They read and . . . friends for life." FW Martin Pope, "A Memory." Accessed 12 Aug. 2019, www.ezra-jack-keats.org/a-memory.

42–43   "Itch worked . . . an ambulance." FF 70.19, 8–9.

43   "Ezra's brother . . . daytime." FF 74.19, 6.

43   "By law . . . regular general." FF 75.02, 14; 75.09, 12.

43–44   "Ezra found . . . other jobs." FF 71.30, 2–5.

44–45   "He worked . . . supper table." BT 76.05; FF 70.04, 1–5; 75.02, 12.

45–49   "Ezra often took . . . real artist." BT 76.02; FF 71.06, 27.

49–50   "To get away . . . on science." BT 76.02; FF 70.01, 6–7; 74.25, 6–7; 75.04, 18.

50–51   "Ezra practiced . . . its collection." FF 75.08, 18; 86.19, Ezra Jack Keats, "Ezra Jack Keats Remembers: Discovering the Library." *Teacher*, Dec. 1976, 40–41.

51   "Mr. Katz called . . . ten-cent store." FF 71.06, 7; 86.17, Freedman, "Brochure of Ezra Jack Keats," 57.

51–52   "By this time . . . bare necessities." FF 70.01, 5; FF 86.19, Ezra Jack Keats, 40–41.

52–53   "On his lunch . . . for all people." FF 70.04, 1–6; 71.13, 11.

53   "Ezra saw . . . it up." BT 76.05.

CHAPTER 5. REFUGE IN HIGH SCHOOL

54–55   "As Ezra entered . . . the window." FF 60.13, article draft; 71.22, 3–4; 86.17, Freedman, "Brochure of Ezra Jack Keats," 57.

55–57   "At home . . . could get it." FF 70.06, 8–11; 86.17, Freedman, "Brochure of Ezra Jack Keats," 57.

57   "Ezra sought . . . Freedman." FF 74.22, 45; 71.06, 12.

57   "Mrs. Freedman . . . she intended." FF 86.17, Freedman, "Brochure of Ezra Jack Keats," 56.

58   "Mrs. Freedman . . . the bully." FF 74.22, 46.

58   "In addition . . . of people." FF 71.15, 1–18.

58–60   "The National Student . . . for the hungry." FF 71.10, 4–7; 74.23, 9–10.

60   "They took hope . . . of America." FF 71.19, 2.

60   "Some nights . . . to iron." BT 76.05; 76.08; FF 74.20, 7.

60–61   "In the meanwhile . . . in his body." BT 76.02; FF 74.24, 7–8.

61   "Giving him the idea . . . of rejection." FF 71.15, 8–10; 74.25, 5.

61–62   "By his final . . . United States." FF 78.08, memorabilia; 78.09, *Liberty Bell*, 28 Mar. 1934; 86.17 Freedman, "Brochure of Ezra Jack Keats," 58.

62–63   "Reaching . . . Max Weber." CF Max Weber, handwritten letter; FF 71.14.

63   "Articles . . . Ostrowsky." FF 78.09.

63   "Neighbors . . . work away." FF 71.06, 12–13.

63   "As Jefferson . . . show up." FF 60.13, article draft; 71.06, 12–13; 71.13, 9; 71.22, 1.

63–65   "At noon . . . tell Mae?" FF 71.22, 1–2; 75.03, 19–20.

65   "The massive . . . secret pride." FF 71.22, 3.

CHAPTER 6. UNCERTAIN DAYS

66–67   "The Katz family . . . the bills." FF 72.04, 1–2.

67   "Kelly planned . . . received." FF 74.19, 1–3; 75.01, 23.

67   "He searched . . . unemployed." FF 72.04, 2.

67–68   "He answered . . . had started." FF 75.02, 1–3.

68   "In the meantime . . . 25 percent unemployment." "Unemployment Statistics for the Great Depression," Croft Communications. Accessed 27 Oct. 2018, http://thegreatdepressioncauses.com/unemployment.

68   "His card . . . New York." FF 79.12, card.

68   "In June . . . urban life." CF Art Students League of New York, letter dated 18 June 1935; Virginia M. Mecklenburg, "Kenneth Hayes Miller." Accessed 26 Jan. 2018, https://americanart.si.edu/artist/kenneth-hayes-miller-3331.

68–69   "Jack's reputation . . . now on." CF Jefferson High School, Bernard I. Green, letter dated 25 July 1935; FF 78.09, undated.

69–71   "Jack found . . . an artist." FF 72.04, 2–5; 75.02, 3–10, 15–18.

71–72   "At home . . . as a child." BT 76.01; FF 74.21, 1C, 2D; 75.01, 33.

72   "During this time . . . art." FF 86.17, Freedman, "Brochure of Ezra Jack Keats,"
           58.
72   "Over the . . . June 1939." FF 78.06, address list.
72–73   "Nighttime found . . . the class." FF 72.05, 5–9.
73–74   "Jack tried . . . fine now." BT 76.02; 76.05; FF 73.12, 1–2, 6–10.
74   "Jack took . . . the people." FF 71.15, 8.
74–75   "Identifying with . . . Jack's memory." FF 75.01, 27–28.
75   "In the meantime . . . other home." Martin and Lillie Pope, telephone
           conversation with the author, 8 July 2011.
75   "Not quite ready . . . to cry." Edna Cain Daniel, "Pictures to the Editors,"
           Life, 13 May 1940, 123.
76   "Jack liked . . . become." FF 60.11, Caldecott speech.
76   "Gradually, . . . captain's face." FF 75.02, 19.
77   "On December . . . Florida." FW Martin Pope.
77–78   "Jack, as he . . . picture." FF 60.09, press release; 75.03, 28–32; 78.11, camouflage
           school certificate.
78   "A good day . . . knew." CF Martin and Lillie Pope, letter dated 17 Dec. 1942.
78–79   "Jack was . . . a week." CF Mae Katz, letter dated 6 Oct. 1945.
79   "Their rabbi . . . difficulties." CF Mae Katz, Rabbi Morton Harris, undated
           letter.
79   "The letters . . . medal." FF 78.12, discharge papers and medal.

CHAPTER 7. LOOKING FOR HIMSELF

80   "In the different world . . . buddies." BT 76.01; FF 74.01.
80   "Jack's childhood . . . condition." FF 78.12, VA correspondence.
80–81   "Soon Itch . . . crackers." Martin Pope, "A Memoir by Martin Pope," Brian
           Alderson, *Ezra Jack Keats: Artist and Picture-Book Maker* (Gretna, LA:
           Pelican Publishing, 1994), 71.
81   "Working in his . . . he said." BT 76.01; FF 74.01, 11.
82   "Jack struck . . . approve." BT 76.01; FF 74.01, 11.
82   "Hoping to . . . last name." FF 78.02, name change documents.
82   "Gussie Katz . . . there." FF 74.21; 76.01.
82–83   "Along with . . . the loan." FF 74.25, 47.
83   "Jack contacted . . . passport." FF 79.05, Acadamie de la Grande Chaumière
           correspondence.
83–85   "In his trip . . . cathedral." CF Rosalie Bolton, diary.
85   "The ship docked . . . dimensional." CF Rosalie Bolton, letter 1, dated 22
           Apr. 1949.
85–87   "He took a . . . Roger's history." BT 76.01; FF 72.08, 1–3.

87–88   "Without delay . . . white." CF Rosalie Bolton, diary.

88   "Soon Jack . . . sculpture." CF Rosalie Bolton, letter 2, dated 10 May 1949.

88   "He walked . . . grave." FF 73.06, 12.

88–89   "War-torn . . . her friends." CF Rosalie Bolton, letter 2.

89–91   "Before his formal . . . Europe." CF Rosalie Bolton, undated letter 3.

91   "One day, Jack . . . painted away." FF 75.06.

91–92   "Soon, he realized . . . to happen." FF 72.08, 10–12.

92   "Jack rehearsed . . . approached." BT 76.01.

93–96   "One afternoon, Jack . . . opened the envelope." FF 72.08, 24–33.

96   "I'm the worst . . . Love, Frederique." CF Frederique, letter.

96   "Roger and Jack . . . des Sports." FF 72.09, 11–12.

96–97   "Jack's fourth . . . again soon." CF Rosalie Bolton, letter 4, dated 11 July 1949.

97–98   "A cable had . . . meadows." Jay Williams, *A Climate of Change* (New York: Random House, 1956), 52–62.

98   "Jack's fifth . . . her letters." CF Rosalie Bolton, letter 5, dated 20 July 1949.

98–99   "His sixth . . . her job." CF Rosalie Bolton, undated letter 6.

99   "The end of . . . you can." CF Rosalie Bolton, letter 7, dated 27 Aug. 1949 and undated letter 8.

99–100   "An undated . . . there." CF Rosalie Bolton, undated letter 9.

100   "In the next . . . New York." CF Rosalie Bolton, undated letter 10.

100–103   "Their trip . . . a lighthouse." FF 74.09, 1–11.

103–4   "When Jack . . . purple suit." FF 74.10, 9.

104–5   "In the morning . . . England." FF 74.10, 11.

105   "He returned . . . landlord." FF 79.02, passport stamps.

105   "Back in New York . . . did it." CF Rosalie Bolton, letter dated Jan 1950.

105   "In an interview . . . having children." BT 76.08.

CHAPTER 8. STARVING ARTIST?

106   "Keats would . . . continued." FF 87.14.

106   "Landlords learned . . . apartment." FF 73.06, 6.

106–7   "One night . . . a show." FF 73.06, 1–9.

107   The Associated . . . Plaza." FF 157.22.

108–9   "Response to . . . his head." FF 73.06, 13–20.

109–10   "In the meantime . . . sales." Brian Alderson, *Ezra Jack Keats: Artist and Picture-Book Maker* (Gretna, LA: Pelican Publishing, 1994), 42.

110   "The Freedmans . . . them." FF 157.26.

110   "Even with the help . . . his habit." FF 74.12, 1.

110   "Bit by bit . . . Morehead City." CF Paul Cleland, letter dated 27 Jan. 1952.

110–11   "Slowly, Jack . . . not last." FF 157.03–157.11, illustration copies.

111	"Mira read . . . his life." FF 73.06, 20–21.

111–15   "After the Easter . . . was finished." FF 60.13, article draft; 73.06, 21–32; 86.17, Freedman, "Brochure of Ezra Jack Keats," 59.

115   "The promise . . . arrived." CF McCain, letters dated 31 Dec. 1953 and 9 Nov. 1954.

115–16   "Returning home . . . brooms." FF 73.06, 32–35.

117   "At home . . . and self-delusion." BT 76.05; FF 73.06, 40–43, 50–51; 74.12, 3; 74.13.

117   "One night . . . to himself." BT 76.05; FF 73.12, 6; 75.01, 16.

118   "Likely giving . . . *Digest*." BT 76.05; FF 60.13, article draft; 74.13, 3; 86.17, Freedman, "Brochure of Ezra Jack Keats," 55; FF 157.14, Silas Marner illustration.

118   "*Jubilant for* . . . the year." FF 86.17, Freedman, "Brochure of Ezra Jack Keats," 59.

118   "Phyllis Whitney . . . traveler." CF Phyllis A. Whitney, letter to John Kelly and Dee Jones, dated 18 Mar. 1985.

118–19   "After his success . . . in books." FF 86.15, Macmillan interview with Keats.

119   "Jack joined . . . beginning." FF 60.13, article draft; 86.17, Freedman, "Brochure of Ezra Jack Keats," 59; Ezra Jack Keats and Pat Cherr, *My Dog Is Lost* (New York: Thomas Y. Crowell, 1960).

CHAPTER 9. A STORY IN THE SNOW

120   "A night, a walk . . . you guys." FF 73.14, 5.

120   "Jack embarked . . . protagonist." FF 60.13, Caldecott speech, 1.

121   "The entire text . . . white." William S. Gray, *Panorama* (Chicago: Scott, Foresman, and Company, 1957).

121   "Jack had . . . was there." FF 86.18, Ezra Jack Keats, "Dear Mr. Keats," *Horn Book Magazine*, June 1972, 306.

121–22   "His art . . . 'Me.'" FF 60.11, Caldecott speech, 1–3; 73.14, 5–6.

122   "He sent . . . Rosalie." FF 60.13, article draft.

122   "Jack was . . . would lead." FF 87.14.

122–24   "About the time . . . your name." FF 73.14, 6–8.

124   "But one paragraph . . . your book goes." CF Ruth Gagliardo, letter dated 6 Feb. 1963.

124–25   "Jack would . . . again." FF 73.14, 8–9.

125   "As time neared . . . luck." FF 60.17 and FF 60.18, T-shirt and briefs.

125   "Finally, the night . . . a hitch." FF 73.14, 6–8.

126   "After the . . . *Time*." FF 60.15.

126   "In his pride . . . and himself." FF 73.14, 11.

126–27   "On his next . . . them up." FF 73.14, 12.

CHAPTER 10. REACTIONS TO *THE SNOWY DAY*

128 "In addition to . . . #182." FF 60.07, *Brooklyn World Telegram*, 20 May 1963, B2.

128 "Several newspapers . . . children." FF 60.07, Charlotte Blount, *Winston-Salem, NC Journal and Sentinel*; *Baltimore Sun*, no date given.

128 "Ezra particularly . . . I do." CF Langston Hughes, letter dated Feb. 18, 1963.

128–29 "In a flowery . . . *Snowy Day*." CF Mrs. James Weldon Johnson, letter dated 14 Apr. 1963.

129–30 Charlemae Rollins . . . celebration." FF 86.07, Charlemae Rollins, "Progress in Children's Books about the Negro." *Illinois Libraries*, Dec. 1963, 544.

130 "An elementary . . . themselves." FF 60.07, *Minneapolis Star*.

130 "Even better . . . carton." FF 86.18, Ezra Jack Keats, 310.

130 "But not all . . . edition." FF 60.07, *Minneapolis Star*.

130–31 "Keats's joyride . . . bandanna." FF 86.30, Nancy Larrick, "The All-White World of Children's Books," *Saturday Review*, 11 Sept. 1965, 63–65, 84–85.

131–32 "Keats did . . . beautiful." FF 86.31, Ezra Jack Keats, "Letters to the Editor," *Saturday Review*, 2 Oct. 1965, 38.

132 "According to his . . . afford." Deborah Pope, conversation with the author.

132–33 "I deplore and detest . . . Connecticut." CF Irene Roop, letter dated 17 Jan. 1965.

133 "Miss Larrick's criticism . . . Washington, DC." CF Keats, "Letters to the Editor," 38.

133–34 "In rebuttal to . . . social research." CF *Saturday Review*, Carole F. Schwartz, letter dated 11 Sept. 1965.

134 "Keats, not . . . thing!" CF *Saturday Review*, Ezra Jack Keats letter to the *Education Review*, 18 Sept. 1965.

134 Larrick responded . . . way he is." CF *Saturday Review*, Nancy Larrick, letter dated 17 Sept. 1965.

134–35 "I have just received . . . from the text." CF *Saturday Review*, Ezra Jack Keats, letter dated 20 Sept. 1965.

135–36 "Ellen Tarry . . . too long." CF *Saturday Review*, Ellen Tarry, letter dated 20 Sept. 1965.

CHAPTER 11. MANY BOOKS

137 "Back in the . . . to Keats." FF 86.18, Ezra Jack Keats, 308.

137 "Soon he was . . . artist." CF Phyllis Whitney, letter to John Kelly and Dee Jones dated 18 Mar. 1985.

138   "Keats's perception . . . sister." Ezra Jack Keats, *Peter's Chair* (New York: Harper Collins, 1967).

138   "Peter struggled . . . things out." Ezra Jack Keats, *A Letter to Amy* (New York: Harper and Row, 1968).

138   "Bullies show . . . childhood." Ezra Jack Keats, *Goggles* (New York: Viking, 1969).

138   "Peter becomes . . . Keats himself." Ezra Jack Keats, *Hi, Cat!* (New York: Macmillan, 1970).

138–39   "When Keats . . . himself." FF 87.15, Macmillan brochure.

139   "Apt. 3 . . . Betsy." Ezra Jack Keats, *Louie* (New York: Macmillan, 1971).

139–40   "Keats watched . . . big hat." Ezra Jack Keats, *Skates!* (New York: Greenwillow, 1978); FF 87.01, interview.

140   "Louie . . . adult Keats." Ezra Jack Keats, *Louie* (New York: Greenwillow, 1978).

140–41   "Louie finds . . . his mother." Ezra Jack Keats, *Louie's Search* (New York: Four Winds Press, 1980).

141   "In the fourth . . . details." Ezra Jack Keats, *Regards to the Man in the Moon* (New York: Four Winds Press, 1981); FW vimeo, https://vimeo .com/58846352.

141   "Ideas for . . . *Hat* (1966)." FF 87.01, unpublished interview notes.

141   "Adding one . . . *Legend* (1965)." Ezra Jack Keats, *John Henry: An American Legend* (New York: Pantheon Books, 1985).

141–42   "God Is . . . EJK." Ezra Jack Keats, *God Is in the Mountain* (New York: Harper and Row, 1966).

142   "Using bright . . . too." FF 70.19, 8. Ezra Jack Keats, *The Little Drummer Boy* (New York: Macmillan, 1968).

142   "Night . . . lettering." Ezra Jack Keats, *Night* (New York: Atheneum, 1969).

142–43   "Taking the traditional . . . animals." Ezra Jack Keats, *Over in the Meadow* (New York: Four Winds Press, 1971).

143   "Ezra had almost . . . style." CF Simon and Schuster, contracts and legal work, 1970–1983); Lynn Hamilton, "The Story of a Quest to Be Free." Accessed 8 July 2011, http://articles.philly.com/1991-02-17/news/25774516_1_ellen-craft -william-craft-freedom.

143   "In what . . . and Deborah." Ezra Jack Keats, *Clementina's Cactus* (New York: Viking, 1982).

143   "Keats described . . . the story." FF 87.01, unpublished interview notes.

CHAPTER 12. THE JAPANESE CONNECTION

145   "As children in . . . kyu, kyu, kyu." FF 86.18, Ezra Jack Keats, 310.

145–48 "Japan became . . . learned English." CF Sachiko Saionj, original correspondence; FF 73.16, 12; 86.21, "Ezra Jack Keats," *Publishers' Weekly*, 16 July 1973.

148–50 "An unexpected . . . to Akira." FF 73.16, 12–18; CF Tashiko Ishida, original correspondence.

CHAPTER 13. MANY LETTERS, MANY ROADS

151 "After his books . . . appalling." CF Viking Press, letter to Velma Varner dated 3 June 1969.

151 "In a turnaround . . . again." CF Viking Press, letter from Velma Varner dated 9 June 1969.

151–52 "Keats particularly . . . cramp." FF 86.18, Ezra Jack Keats, 307.

152 "Keats answered . . . did, too." CF Essex Co. School Library Association, letter dated 18 Nov. 1968.

152 "One letter . . . painting." CF Paul Cleland, letter dated 23 Mar. 1980.

152 "Keats answered . . . the area." CF Paul Cleland, letter dated 11 May 1980.

152 "Keats wrote . . . Jack." CF Bonnie Keats correspondence.

153 "One day . . . books." Alderson, *Ezra Jack Keats*, 64; FF 117.08.

153 "With a keen . . . Anna." CF Bibliotekstjanst, letter dated 72-03-34.

153 "Another request for . . . been sent." CF Paul Brandes correspondence.

153 "detailed discussions . . . books." CF Weston Woods correspondence.

153 "He received . . . book." CF *Who's Who in America*.

153 "Ursula Nordstrom . . . hate her." Leonard S. Marcus, *Dear Genius: The Letters of Ursula Nordstrom* (New York: HarperCollins, 1998), 218–19.

153 "Assorted mail . . . Television." CF Children's Television Network.

153–54 "response from . . . Associates." CF Jim Henson, letter dated 27 Jan. 1971.

154 "A letter . . . classes." CF Martin and Lillie Pope, letter dated 25 Aug. 1974.

154–55 "The US Information . . . future." CF US Information Agency, letter dated 10 Oct. 1967.

155 "With an international . . . a year." CF UNICEF correspondence 1965–1982.

155 "Success . . . card line." CF American Artist Group, letter dated 12 Apr. 1967.

155–56 "Lloyd N. Morrisett . . . stations." CF Children's Television Network including letter dated 19 June 1968, seminar schedule, and list of participants; "Cooney, Joan Ganz: U.S. Producer/Media Executive." Accessed 3 May 2010, http://www .museum.tv/eotvsection.php?entrycode=cooneyjoan.

156 "In similar . . . children." CF Lynda Johnson Robb correspondence, 20 May 1968–3 Feb. 1982.

156–57 "In a news release . . . Manhattan." CF Greenwillow Books, letter to Mr. Daniel Posnansky at Harvard dated 23 Apr. 1976; CF Harvard University, letter dated 30 Dec. 1969; FF 86.05; 86.06.

157–58   "Not shy . . . conclusion." CF Bruno Bettelheim. Keats and Bettelheim letter exchange. An interesting follow-up to the doctor occurs in a footnote in *The Autistic Brain* by Temple Grandin, "In the decade following Bettelheim's death in 1990, his reputation unraveled. Evidence emerged that he had misrepresented his education, plagiarized, conducted shoddy research, and lied about being a doctor, but even more damning were accusations of physical and mental abuse by former students at the Orthogenic School" (New York: Mariner Books, 2014), 8.

158   "Beginning . . . lives." FF 86.10; 86.11; CF Mister Rogers Neighborhood; http:// www.neighborhoodarchive.com/mrn/episodes/1164/index.html; http://www .neighborhoodarchive.com/mrn/episodes/1252/index.html; http://www .neighborhoodarchive.com/mrn/episodes/1330/index.html; Keats picture book explanation on Mr. Rogers, https://youtu.be/qPmnGvFA8P0; Keats and Mr. Rogers making marbleized paper, https://youtu.be/aTJRbmOhjoU.

158–59   "In 1972 . . . morning." CF Syd Hoff, letters dated 27 Mar. 1972 and 12 Apr. 1972.

159   "Keats's scribbled . . . children." CF Syd Hoff, undated letter from Ezra.

159   "Macmillan, in . . . working for." CF Macmillan, correspondence; Janet Schulman, "Looking Back: The 1974 Macmillan Massacre." Accessed 17 Feb. 2011, https://publishersweekly.com/pw/by-topic/childrens/childrens-industry -news/article/15635-looking-back-the-1974-macmillan-massacre.html.

159–60   "The Society . . . generous." CF Society of Children's Book Writers correspondence; Stephen Mooser, email to the author, 9 Jan. 2019.

160   "After his books . . . Freedman." FF 95.19–95.22, travel to Israel.

160   "A trip to . . . coat." FF 71.19, 3.

160   "No matter . . . to him." FF 60.13, article draft.

160   "Keats received . . . Colorado." FF 84.

160–61   "He was . . . Iran." FF 94, Travels to Tehran.

161   "One special . . . books." CF Kaisei-Sha Publishing, letter dated 6 June 1979.

161   "No matter . . . Itch." FF 80.01, appointment books for 1963, 1968, and 1972.

161   "Between trips . . . to supervise." CF Donald Bratman; FF 118.02, publicity photo.

161   "Ezra enjoyed . . . delight." FF 87.12, talk typescript.

161   "Dear Mr. Keats . . . child." FF 86.18, Ezra Jack Keats, 310.

161–62   "He used . . . connections." FF 87.12, typescript.

162   "He felt . . . form." FF 86.18, Ezra Jack Keats, 307, 309.

163   "Herman Goliob . . . Goliob." CF Atheneum Publishers.

163   "His autobiography . . . much." CF Kaisei-Sha Publishing, letter dated 9 Nov. 1976.

163–64   "In a January . . . of him." CF Beverly Hall, letter dated 2 Jan. 1981.

164–66 "Questions from . . . Jack Keats." FF 70.01, 8–9; 86.19, Ezra Jack Keats, 40–41.

166 "Keats continued . . . death." FW Martin Pope.

166 "Keats's weak . . . 1980." CF Patsy Perritt, letter dated 6 Dec. 1967.

166–67 "He recovered . . . archives." CF Onva Broshears, letter from Keats dated 14 Apr. 1980.

167 "Two years later . . . home." Jane Ridley, "Ezra Jack Keats and 'The Snowy Day' are honored on book's 50th anniversary," *New York Daily News*, published 13 Nov. 2011. Accessed 14 Nov. 2011, www.nydailynews.com/entertainment/ezra-jack-keats-snowy-day-honored-book-50th-anniversary-article-1.975036.

AFTERWORD

168 "Martin Pope had instructions . . . the winds." CF Ezra Jack Keats, Ezra Jack Keats to Moser and Henkin, Counselors at Law, 31 Aug. 1982.

168 "The Ezra Jack Keats Foundation . . . the task." FW "A History of the Ezra Jack Keats Foundation." Accessed 20 Nov. 2018, www.ezra-jack-keats.org/a-history-of-the-ezra-jack-keats-foundation.

168–69 "Dr. Martin Pope . . . programs." FW "Dr. Martin Pope: Founder." Accessed 20 Nov. 2018, www.ezra-jack-keats.org/staff.

169 "In the ensuing years, the Pope family . . . Keats." FW "Ezra Jack Keats Mini-Grants." Accessed 7 Feb. 2019, www.ezra-jack-keats.org/section/ezra-jack-keats-mini-grant-program-for-public-libraries-public-schools.

169 "In an early program . . . in 1992." FF 0167, Ezra Jack Keats Award Memorial Program.

169–70 "Hannah Nuba, proposed . . . writers." FW "A History of the Ezra Jack Keats Foundation."

170 "With these Writer and . . . careers." FW "EJK Award." Accessed 5 Aug. 2019, www.ezra-jack-keats.org/section/ezra-jack-keats-book-awards.

170 "The Popes have . . . depot." FW "EJK Award—FAQ." Accessed 6 Aug. 2019, www.ezra-jack-keats.org/faq/faq-book-award.

170 "Dr. Deborah Pope . . . in 1986." FW "Dr. Deborah Pope: Executive Director." Accessed 20 Nov. 2018, www.ezra-jack-keats.org/staff.

171 "Initially instituted with . . . Atlanta." FW "About the Bookmaking Competition." Accessed 7 Feb. 2019, www.ezra-jack-keats.org/h/about-the-bookmaking-competition.

171 "The Ezra Jack Keats minigrant . . . programs." FW "About Mini-Grants." Accessed 24 Nov. 1918, www.ezra-jack-keats.org/h/about-mini-grants.

171 "Taking advantage of . . . composition." FW "Press Release: Emmy Nods for The Snowy Day." Accessed 5 Jan. 2019, www.ezra-jack-keats.org/press-release/press-release-emmy-nods-for-the-snowy-day.

171–72   "Another of her campaigns . . . 'forever' stamps." Ron Charles, "How 'The Snowy Day'—on a Postage Stamp—Can Help Us Rethink Race in America." *Washington Post*, 6 Sept. 2017.

172   "The *New York Times* . . . view." FF 65.00, *New York Times*, 11 Dec. 1983.

172   "Prospect Park Alliance . . . Landmark." "Peter and Willie: History." Accessed 15 Jan. 2019, www.nycgovparks.org/parks/B073/monuments/1915.

172–73   "Bryan Collier . . . *Snowy Day*." Bryan Collier, keynote address. Society of Children's Book Writers and Illustrators Summer Conference, 3 Aug. 2012.

173   "A yearlong observation . . . 2013." Robert Gluck, "The Jewish Artist Who Painted a Picture of Diversity." JointMedia News Service. Accessed 6 Aug. 2019, www .archive.jns.org/latest . . . /9/20/the-jewish-artist-who-painted-a-picture-of -diversity.html.

173–74   "Eric Carle . . . spirit." Eric Carle, "Ezra Jack Keats." Eric Carle's blog. Accessed 24 Oct. 2018, http://ericcarleblog.blogspot.com/2012/07/ezra-jack-keats .html.

174   "The day 2 June 2015 . . . Morrison." FW "Press Release: Emmy Nods for The Snowy Day."

174   "Keats and The Snowy Day . . . Jack Keats." "Michelle Obama: By the Book." *New York Times*. Published 6 Dec. 2018. Accessed 11 Jan. 2019, www.nytimes .com/2018/12/06/books/review/michelle-obama-by-the-book.html.

174   Michelle H. Martin . . . portrayal." Michelle H. Martin, "Black Kids Camp, Too . . . Don't They?: Embracing Wildness in Books," *Horn Book Magazine*, Sept./Oct. 2019, 18.

$\mathcal{B}$IBLIOGRAPHY

ORIGINAL SOURCES

The most important resources for this book have come from the de Grummond Children's Literature Collection at the University of Southern Mississippi, which houses the Ezra Jack Keats archives. While I examined minutely the contents of 167 archival boxes and 13 additional boxes of miscellaneous materials, I gave particular attention to the following:

Three large boxes of correspondence files
Box 0060—Materials surrounding *The Snowy Day*
Boxes 0070–0075—Autobiographical writings of Ezra Jack Keats (EJK), unfinished
    and unpublished
Box 0076—Tapes of EJK telling stories about his life
    Some of these tapes are transcribed and in the autobiographical materials, but
    the transcriber did not record as painstakingly as I would have liked. I was able
    to listen and do my own transcriptions until I broke two tapes. The special
    collections people and I agreed they were too fragile to continue.

Telephone conversations and interviews with people who knew EJK:
Jeannine Laughlin-Porter, director of the USM Children's Book Festival in 1980,
    when EJK received its Medallion—at various times during the past fifteen years
Deborah Pope, current director of the Ezra Jack Keats Foundation and daughter
    of his lifelong friend Martin Pope—15 June 2011; 24 Apr. 2014; several personal
    conversations at the annual Fay B. Kaigler Children's Book Festival and Ezra
    Jack Keats Awards Event.

Martin and Lillie Pope, lifelong friends of EJK and first director of the Keats Foundation—7 July 2011; 16 Sept. 2011

Visit to Brooklyn Public Library, Arlington Branch—12 Sept. 2011

SECONDARY SOURCES

Books

Alderson, Brian. *Ezra Jack Keats: Artist and Picture-Book Maker*. Gretna, LA: Pelican Publishing, 1994, and using the following article:
• Pope, Martin. "A Memoir by Martin Pope."
Alderson, Brian. *Ezra Jack Keats: A Bibliography and Catalog*. Gretna, LA: Pelican Publishing, 2002.
Chametzky, Jules. *From the Ghetto: The Fiction of Abraham Cahan*. Amherst: University of Massachusetts Press, 1977.
Children's Authors Speak. Edited by Jeannine Laughlin and Sherry Laughlin. Englewood, CA: Libraries Unlimited, 1993, using the following articles:
• Butler, Dorothy. "Saying It Louder Still."
• Laughlin, Jeannine L. "An Interview with Ezra Jack Keats."
• Laughlin, Jeannine L. "Introduction."
• Thwaite, Ann. "Expecting the Best."
Dowling, Robert M. *Slumming in New York: From the Waterfront to Mythic Harlem*. Urbana: University of Illinois Press, 2007.
Engel, Dean, and Florence Freedman. *Ezra Jack Keats: A Biography with Illustrations*. New York: Silver Moon Press, 1995.
Finkelstein, Normal L. *Three Across: The Great Transatlantic Air Race of 1927*. Honesdale, PA: Calkins Creek/Boyds Mills Press, 2008.
Grandin, Temple. *The Autistic Brain*. New York: Mariner Books, 2014.
Gray, William S. *Panorama*. Chicago: Scott, Foresman, and Company, 1957.
Keats, Ezra Jack. *Apt. 3*. New York: Macmillan, 1971.
Keats, Ezra Jack. *Clementina's Cactus*. New York: Viking, 1982.
Keats, Ezra Jack. *Dreams*. New York: Macmillan, 1974.
Keats, Ezra Jack. *God Is in the Mountain*. New York: Holt, Rinehart and Winston, 1966.
Keats, Ezra Jack. *Goggles*. New York: Macmillan, 1969.
Keats, Ezra Jack. *Hi, Cat!* New York: Macmillan, 1970.
Keats, Ezra Jack. *Jennie's Hat*. New York: Harper and Row, 1966.
Keats, Ezra Jack. *John Henry: An American Legend*. New York: Pantheon Books, 1985.
Keats, Ezra Jack. *Kitten for a Day*. New York: Four Winds Press, 1974.
Keats, Ezra Jack. *A Letter to Amy*. New York: Harper and Row, 1968.

Keats, Ezra Jack. *The Little Drummer Boy*. New York: Macmillan, 1968.

Keats, Ezra Jack. *Louie*. New York: Greenwillow, 1975.

Keats, Ezra Jack. *Louie's Search*. New York: Four Winds Press, 1980.

Keats, Ezra Jack. *Maggie and the Pirate*. New York: Four Winds Press, 1979.

Keats, Ezra Jack. *Night*. New York: Atheneum, 1969.

Keats, Ezra Jack. *Over in the Meadow*. New York: Four Winds Press, 1971.

Keats, Ezra Jack. *Pet Show*. New York: Macmillan, 1972.

Keats, Ezra Jack. *Peter's Chair*. New York: Harper and Row, 1967.

Keats, Ezra Jack. *Psst! Doggie-*. New York: Franklin Watts, 1973.

Keats, Ezra Jack. *Regards to the Man in the Moon*. New York: Four Winds Press, 1981.

Keats, Ezra Jack. *Skates!* New York: Franklin Watts, 1973.

Keats, Ezra Jack. *The Snowy Day*. New York: Viking, 1962.

Keats, Ezra Jack. *The Trip*. New York: Greenwillow, 1978.

Keats, Ezra Jack. *Whistle for Willie*. New York: Viking, 1964.

Keats, Ezra Jack, and Pat Cherr. *My Dog Is Lost*. New York: Thomas Y. Crowell, 1960.

Marcus, Leonard S. *Dear Genius: The Letters of Ursula Nordstrom*. New York: Harper Collins, 1998.

Nahson, Claudia J. *The Snowy Day and the Art of Ezra Jack Keats*. New Haven, CT: Yale University Press, 2011.

Singer, Isaac Bashevis. *In My Father's Court*. New York: Farrar, Straus, and Giroux, 1966.

Taylor, Sydney. *All-of-a-Kind Family*. New York: Wilcox and Follett, 1951.

Williams, Jay. *A Climate of Change*. New York: Random House, 1956.

Magazines

Clough, G. Wayne. "Big Opportunity." *Smithsonian Magazine*, November 2010, 28.

Daniel, Edna Cain. "Pictures to the Editors." *Life*, 13 May 1940, 123.

"Ezra Jack Keats." *Publishers' Weekly*, 16 July 1973.

"Ezra Jack Keats: the Consummate Artist." *Early Years*, 23, 103, 105. [Appears to be excerpts of an interview with editors with no date and no attribution listed]

Keats, Ezra Jack. "Dear Mr. Keats, ..." *Horn Book Magazine*, June 1972, 306–10.

Keats, Ezra Jack. "Ezra Jack Keats Remembers: Discovering the Library." *Teacher*, Dec. 1976, 40–41.

Keats, Ezra Jack. "Letters to the Editor." *Saturday Review*, 2 Oct. 1965.

Larrick, Nancy. "The All-White World of Children's Books." *Saturday Review*, 11 Sept. 1965, 63–65, 85. [And Keats's and others' replies in the 16 Oct. edition]

Martin, Michelle H. "Black Kids Camp, Too . . . Don't They?: Embracing Wildness in Books." *Horn Book Magazine*, Sept./Oct. 2019, 18.

Rollins, Charlemae. "Progress in Children's Books about the Negro." *Illinois Libraries*, Dec. 1963.

Rose, Helen Nemetz. "Children's Picture Books Teach Teachers, Too." *Elementary English* 51, Mar. 1976, 337–40.

Newspapers

Charles, Ron. "How 'The Snowy Day'—on a Postage Stamp—Can Help Us Rethink Race in America." *Washington Post*, 6 Sept. 2017.

Other

Collier, Bryan. Keynote address. Society of Children's Book Writers and Illustrators Summer Conference, 3 Aug. 2012.

Fox, Vicki Reikes, and Rabbi Uri Barnea. "From the Outside Looking In: Telling Stories through a Personal Lens." *The World of Maurice Sendak: In a Nutshell.* Presentation and exhibition by the de Grummond Children's Literature Collection, 9 July 2011 and 11 Aug. 2011.

Freedman, Florence B. *Ezra Jack Keats; Author and Illustrator.* [Brochure reprinted from *Elementary English*, Jan. 1969, 55–65. Copyright by National Council of Teachers of English]

Jones, Dee. *Collage: An Ezra Jack Keats Retrospective.* [Catalog written for an exhibition running January through July 2002]

Joseph, Samuel. *Jewish Immigration to the United States from 1881 to 1910.* New York: Arno Press and New York Times, 1969. [Doctoral dissertation for Columbia University, 1914]

Internet Sources

American Heritage Magazine. 43, no. 2, Apr. 1992. http://www.americanheritage.com/articles/magazine/ah/1992/2/1992_2_56_print.shtml.

Bennett, Anita. "The Art of Comic Book Inking" (rewrite). 14 Feb. 2011. http://www.bigredhair.com/work/writing_samples/InkingBook.pdf.

Bilitsky, John. "Memories of ENY Brooklyn." The Brooklyn Board. 29 May 2014. http://brooklynboard.com/diary/diary.php?f-Memories+of+ENY+Brooklyn.

Blanck, Maggie Land. "Immigration Photos and Pictures." 5 July 2011. http://www.maggieblanck.com/Immigration.html.

"Brownsville, Brooklyn." Wikipedia Online. 21 Sept. 2010. http://en.wikipedia.org/wiki/Brownsville_Brooklyn.

Carle, Eric. "Ezra Jack Keats." Eric Carle's blog. 24 Oct. 2018. http://ericcarleblog.blogspot.com/2012/07/ezra-jack-keats.html.

"Cooney, Joan Ganz: U. S. Producer/Media Executive." 3 May 2010. http://www.museum.tv/eotvsection.php?entrycode=cooneyjoan.

"Dybbuk." *Encyclopedia Britannica*. Encyclopedia Britannica Online. 21 Sept. 2010. http://www.britannica.com/EBchecked/topic/174964/dybbuk.

"Dybbuk—Spiritual Possession and Jewish Folklore." Ghost Village.com. 21 Sept. 2010. http://www.ghostvillage.com/legends/2003/legends32_11292003.shtml.

"Ezra Jack Keats Biography." The de Grummond Children's Literature Collection. 20 Apr. 2010. http://www.lib.usm.edu/~degrum/keats/biography.html.

Ezra Jack Keats Foundation. "About the Bookmaking Competition." 7 Feb. 2019. www.ezra-jack-keats.org/h/about-the-bookmaking-competition.

Ezra Jack Keats Foundation. "About Mini-Grants." 24 Nov. 1918. www.ezra-jack-keats.org/h/about-mini-grants.

Ezra Jack Keats Foundation. "Dr. Deborah Pope: Executive Director." 20 Nov. 2018. www.ezra-jack-keats.org/staff.

Ezra Jack Keats Foundation. "Dr. Martin Pope: Founder." 20 Nov. 2018. www.ezra-jack-keats.org/staff.

Ezra Jack Keats Foundation. "EJK Award." 5 Aug. 2019. www.ezra-jack-keats.org/section/ezra-jack-keats-book-awards.

Ezra Jack Keats Foundation. "EJK Award—FAQ." 6 Aug. 2019. www.ezra-jack-keats.org/faq/faq-book-award.

Ezra Jack Keats Foundation. "Ezra Jack Keats Mini-Grants." 7 Feb. 2019. www.ezra-jack-keats.org/section/ezra-jack-keats-mini-grant-program-for-public-libraries-public-schools.

Ezra Jack Keats Foundation. "A History of the Ezra Jack Keats Foundation." 20 Nov. 2018. www.ezra-jack-keats.org/a-history-of-the-ezra-jack-keats-foundation.

Ezra Jack Keats Foundation. "Press Release: Emmy Nods for The Snowy Day." 5 Jan. 2019. www.ezra-jack-keats.org/press-release/press-release-emmy-nods-for-the-snowy-day.

Gluck, Robert. "The Jewish Artist Who Painted a Picture of Diversity." JointMedia News Service. 6 Aug. 2019. www.archive.jns.org/latest . . . /9/20/the-jewish-artist-who-painted-a-picture-of-diversity.html.

"Great Depression." History Channel. 26 Jan. 2018. http://www.history.com/topics/great-depression.

Hamilton, Lynn. "The Story of a Quest to Be Free." 8 July 2011. http://articles.philly.com/1991-02-17/news/25774516_1_ellen-craft-william-craft-freedom.

"Harry A. Chesler." Wikipedia Online. 29 Jan. 2018. https://en.wikipedia.org/wiki/Harry_"A"_Chesler.

"The Hebrew Letters—Tzadik: The Faith of the Righteous One." Gai Enai Institute, Inc. 6 July 2011. http://www.inner.org/hebleter/tzadik.htm.

"Indian Clubs." *New England Antiques Journal*. 15 Oct. 2010. http://www.antiquesjournal.com/pages04/archives/indianclubs.html.

"The Jazz Age: The American 1920s." *Digital History*. 25 Sept. 2011. http://digitalhistory
.uh.edu/database/article_display.cfm?HHID+441.

Kabbalah in Ohio. "What Is the Definition of a Righteous Person?" 6 July 2011. http://
www.facebook.com/note.php?note_id+191253070905506.

Kennedy, Elizabeth. "The Magic of Ezra Jack Keats." About.com. 20 Apr. 2010. http://
childrensbooks.about.com/cs/authorsillustrato/a/ezrajackkeats.htm.

Lee, Dan P. "Peaches: Who's Your Daddy?" The History of New York Scandals—
Peaches Browning's Acid Attack. *New York Magazine*. 17 Oct. 2018. http://nymag
.com/news/features/scandals/peaches-browning-2012-4/index1.html.

Mecklenburg, Virginia M. "Kenneth Hayes Miller." 26 Jan. 2018. https://americanart
.si.edu/artist/kenneth-hayes-miller-3331.

Mohl, Nachum. "Be a Tzadik, Be a Mensch." *Jewish Magazine*. 6 Jul. 2011. http://www
.jewishmag.com/86mag/benoni/benoni.htm.

Neighborhood Archive—All Things Mister Rogers. Episode 1164. http://www.neigh
borhoodarchive.com/mrn/episodes/1164/index.html.

Neighborhood Archive—All Things Mister Rogers. Episode 1252. http://www.neigh
borhoodarchive.com/mrn/episodes/1252/index.html.

Neighborhood Archive—All Things Mister Rogers. Episode 1330. http://www.neigh
borhoodarchive.com/mrn/episodes/1330/index.html.*New York Times*. "Michelle
Obama: By the Book." 6 Dec. 2018. www.nytimes.com/2018/12/06/books/review/
michelle-obama-by-the-book.html.

"Old Staten Island—Staten Island History." 19 Sept. 2011. http://www.statenisland
history.com.

"Peter and Willie: History." 15 Jan. 2019. https://www.nycgovparks.org/parks/B073/
monuments/1915.

"Phyllis A. Whitney: The Official Website." 13 Jan. 2011. http://www.phylliswhitney
.com.

"Picasso's Classicism and Surrealism Period—1918 to 1945." Pablo Picasso and His
Paintings. 25 July 2011. http://www.pablopicasso.org/pablo-picasso-classicism
-period.jsp.

Pope, Martin. "A Memory." 12 Aug. 2019. www.ezra-jack-keats.org/a-memory.

Ridley, Jane. "Ezra Jack Keats and 'The Snowy Day' are honored on book's 50th anniversary." *New York Daily News*. 13 Nov. 2011. www.nydailynews.com/entertainment/
ezra-jack-keats-snowy-day-honored-book-50th-anniversary-article-1.975036.

Schulman, Janet. "Looking Back: The 1974 Macmillan Massacre." *Publishers Weekly
Online*. 17 Feb. 2011. https://publishersweekly.com/pw/by-topic/childrens/child
rens-industry-news/article/15635-looking-back-the-1974-macmillan-massacre
.html.

"Unemployment Statistics for the Great Depression." The Great Depression. 26 Jan.
2018. http://thegreatdepressioncauses.com/unemployment.

Urban Dictionary. 19 Nov. 2010. http://www.urbandictionary.com/define.php?term =clochard.

Whitmarsh, H. Phelps. "Steerage Conditions in 1898—A First-Hand Account." 5 July 2011. http://www.gjenvick.com/Steerage/1898-SteerageConditions-A PersonalExprience.html.

$\mathcal{I}$NDEX

$\mathcal{A}$BOUT THE $\mathcal{A}$UTHOR

Photograph courtesy of Lauren Damaskinos

Virginia McGee Butler's education began in Mississippi public schools and continued at Itawamba Community College and the University of Mississippi, where she earned an English education degree. Discovery of a love for young children brought her to a master's degree in early childhood education at Incarnate Word University in San Antonio, Texas. For yet another interest, she completed certification in gifted education at Northwestern State University in Natchitoches, Louisiana.

Moves with her military husband and three children enriched her life in six states and three overseas countries. After a rewarding three-decade teaching career in kindergarten, second grade, and junior high in Texas, West Germany, Louisiana, and Mississippi, she retired to Hattiesburg, Mississippi, to write. Involvement with the University of Southern Mississippi brought opportunities to teach writing to students in the Karnes Center for Gifted Studies and to the de Grummond Children's Literature Collection, where she became the researcher for the fiftieth-anniversary edition of *The Snowy Day*.

Her published work has appeared in *Highlights*, *Cricket*, *Thema*, *The Writer*, *The SCBWI Bulletin*, and other publications. Writing her blog, *Readin', 'Ritin, but Not Much 'Rithmetic*, on her website at www.virginiamcgeebutler.com, is therapy for inevitable rejection letters.